ChatGPT Cashflow

Build Your Own Artificial Intelligence, Passive Income Empire On Autopilot

Introduction

"Can you imagine earning money while you sleep? What if you could unlock a powerful tool that could generate passive income, granting you financial freedom and independence? Meet ChatGPT, the cutting-edge language model that has revolutionized the way we interact with technology and opened up new doors for generating income in the digital age."

In today's fast-paced world, where technological advancements are reshaping industries at an unprecedented rate, opportunities to create passive income streams have never been more accessible. Gone are the days when traditional 9-to-5 jobs were the only means of earning a living. With the advent of artificial intelligence and natural language processing, we now find ourselves standing at the threshold of an exciting new era.

This book, "ChatGPT Passive Income Playbook: Harnessing ChatGPT's Secrets for Financial Freedom," is your gateway to understanding and leveraging the incredible potential of ChatGPT. Whether you're a seasoned entrepreneur looking to diversify your income or someone exploring novel avenues for financial stability, ChatGPT has something to offer for everyone.

The concept of passive income isn't new, but with ChatGPT, the game has changed entirely. Unlike traditional methods of generating passive income that might require substantial investments or physical resources, ChatGPT offers a unique opportunity to monetize your creativity, knowledge, and expertise. Through this book, we will explore the multifaceted ways in which ChatGPT can empower you to create sustainable passive income streams.

You might be wondering, "What exactly is ChatGPT?" In simple terms, ChatGPT is an advanced language model developed by OpenAI, designed to understand and generate human-like text based on the input it receives. It's an artificial intelligence marvel that has been trained on vast amounts of data from the internet, books, and various other sources, allowing it to comprehend diverse topics and respond to queries with impressive accuracy and coherence.

The magic of ChatGPT lies in its versatility. From drafting emails and generating content to providing personalized recommendations and even creating conversational agents, its capabilities are far-reaching. As you delve into the pages of this playbook, you will not only understand how ChatGPT works but also discover how you can leverage it to achieve financial abundance.

Throughout this journey, we will explore numerous use cases of ChatGPT in the context of passive income generation. You will uncover the secrets of maximizing ChatGPT's potential to create valuable content that attracts audiences and keeps them engaged. By learning how to tap into the power of this language model, you will gain insights into various online platforms and strategies that can transform your digital presence into a lucrative source of income.

While the possibilities with ChatGPT are immense, it's essential to remember that success requires effort, dedication, and continuous learning. This book aims to equip you with the knowledge, tools, and best practices necessary to make the most of ChatGPT's capabilities effectively.

Before we embark on this transformative journey, it's crucial to acknowledge the ethical considerations surrounding AI and language models. As ChatGPT becomes increasingly integrated into our lives, questions about data privacy, biases, and responsible usage arise. Throughout this book, we will emphasize the importance of ethical practices and guide you in ensuring your ChatGPT applications are conducted in a responsible and conscientious manner.

Now is the time to embrace the boundless possibilities offered by ChatGPT. Whether you're an aspiring digital entrepreneur, content creator, or business owner seeking to enhance your online presence, "ChatGPT Passive Income Playbook: Harnessing ChatGPT's Secrets for Financial Freedom" will serve as your comprehensive guide to achieving your financial goals and unlocking the doors to a more secure and prosperous future.

Are you ready to harness the power of ChatGPT and embark on a journey toward financial freedom? Let's dive in together!

1. Introduction to Passive Income

In this journey toward achieving financial independence, we will delve into the world of passive income and explore how you can leverage the power of ChatGPT to unlock a realm of opportunities.

Imagine waking up to find money flowing into your bank account effortlessly, even as you sleep or spend quality time with your loved ones. That's the allure of passive income - the ability to earn money with minimal ongoing effort. Unlike traditional active income, where you exchange your time and labor for a paycheck, passive income empowers you to build streams of revenue that work for you, freeing up your time and energy for pursuits that truly matter to you.

In this chapter, we will lay the foundation for your passive income journey. We'll begin by understanding what passive income truly means and debunking some common misconceptions about it.

Passive income is not a "get-rich-quick" scheme or a guarantee of instant wealth. Instead, it requires dedication, effort, and patience in the initial stages of setting up your income streams. However, once the groundwork is laid, the rewards can be truly life-changing.

The power of ChatGPT lies in its ability to assist you in generating passive income ideas, guiding you through the process, and providing insights to optimize and scale your endeavors. As an AI language model, ChatGPT is an invaluable tool to help you navigate the complexities of passive income generation and make well-informed decisions.

In the following chapters, we'll explore various passive income strategies, each with its own set of advantages and considerations. From starting an online business, creating digital products, investing in real estate, or even building an affiliate marketing empire, the possibilities are vast and diverse.

Before diving into the practical aspects of passive income, it's essential to address the mindset required to embark on this journey. Shifting from the traditional employee mindset to that of an entrepreneur and investor is crucial. You'll need to embrace a mindset of creativity, adaptability, and resilience to overcome challenges along the way.

One of the keys to success is recognizing that passive income does not happen overnight. It takes time to build sustainable income streams, and setbacks are part of the learning process. However, by leveraging the knowledge and insights offered by ChatGPT, you'll be better equipped to overcome obstacles and stay focused on your goals.

The Role Of AI And Chatgpt In Generating Passive Income

The role of AI, specifically ChatGPT, in generating passive income is revolutionary and transformative. Traditionally, the process of creating passive income streams required extensive research, trial and error, and often a significant investment of time and resources. However, with the advent of AI technologies like ChatGPT, the landscape has drastically changed, offering new possibilities and opportunities for individuals seeking financial freedom.

Idea Generation: One of the most significant contributions of ChatGPT is its ability to assist in generating passive income ideas. By leveraging its vast database of information and language processing capabilities, ChatGPT can offer insights into various passive income strategies, from affiliate marketing and digital product creation to dividend investing and real estate ventures. It helps users explore a wide range of options that align with their interests and expertise.

Market Research: In the realm of passive income, market research is crucial to identify profitable niches and target audiences. ChatGPT can assist in conducting market research by analyzing trends, identifying consumer preferences, and suggesting potential gaps in the market that users can exploit. This information is invaluable in making informed decisions about which income streams to pursue.

Business Planning: ChatGPT can help users with business planning by providing guidance on setting up online businesses, including recommended platforms, marketing strategies, and even pricing strategies for digital products. It can also aid in outlining business plans for various passive income models, highlighting potential risks and suggesting ways to mitigate them.

Content Creation: Quality content is essential for many passive income strategies, such as blogging, content marketing, and YouTube channels. ChatGPT can assist in content creation by generating blog posts, social media content, video scripts, and more. This capability streamlines content production and allows users to focus on other aspects of their passive income ventures.

Optimization and Scaling: As users progress in their passive income journey, they may seek to optimize and scale their income streams for greater profitability. ChatGPT can provide insights into potential areas for improvement, help analyze data to identify trends, and suggest strategies to scale up successful endeavors.

Financial Insights: Understanding the financial aspects of passive income is crucial for long-term success. ChatGPT can offer guidance on budgeting, tax implications, and investment strategies, ensuring that users make well-informed financial decisions to secure their future.

Personalization: AI technologies like ChatGPT can personalize the guidance they provide based on individual preferences, interests, and goals. This level of customization enables users to receive tailored advice, making their passive income journey more effective and enjoyable.

It's important to note that while ChatGPT is a powerful tool, it is not a substitute for human ingenuity and critical thinking. Its role is to augment and enhance the passive income generation process, offering insights and assistance that complement the user's own expertise and creativity.

AI and ChatGPT have revolutionized the way individuals approach passive income generation. By harnessing the capabilities of this cutting-edge technology, users can explore diverse opportunities, make well-informed decisions, and create sustainable streams of income that lead to financial freedom and a more fulfilling life.

2. The Fundamentals of ChatGPT

At its core, ChatGPT is an advanced language model developed by OpenAI. It belongs to the GPT (Generative Pre-trained Transformer) family, which leverages the transformer architecture to process and generate human-like text. Trained on a vast corpus of diverse texts, ChatGPT is equipped with an extensive knowledge base, covering a wide range of topics and subject matters up to its knowledge cutoff date in September 2021.

Natural Language Processing (NLP):

ChatGPT's primary function is to process and generate natural language text. NLP, the field of artificial intelligence that focuses on language understanding and generation, enables ChatGPT to comprehend and respond to human queries and prompts. Its ability to grasp context, syntax, and semantics allows for more accurate and contextually relevant responses.

How ChatGPT Generates Text:

ChatGPT's text generation process is based on its training data and the patterns it learned during training. Given a prompt, ChatGPT uses the transformer architecture to break down the input text into tokens and processes them in parallel. It predicts the most likely next token based on the context provided by the previous tokens. By repeating this process, ChatGPT generates coherent and contextually appropriate responses.

Limitations of ChatGPT:

While ChatGPT is a remarkable AI language model, it does have certain limitations. For instance, it can sometimes produce responses that sound plausible but are factually incorrect or misleading. It may also be sensitive to slight changes in the input phrasing, leading to inconsistent responses. It's essential to be mindful of these limitations and use critical thinking when interpreting ChatGPT's responses.

Interacting with ChatGPT:

Interacting with ChatGPT is relatively straightforward. Users provide prompts or questions, and ChatGPT generates responses based on its training data and language understanding. Throughout this playbook, we'll be utilizing ChatGPT to assist in exploring passive income strategies, business ideas, content creation, and financial insights.

Leveraging ChatGPT for Passive Income:

As we progress, you'll learn how to leverage ChatGPT's capabilities to generate passive income ideas, conduct market research, refine business plans, optimize content creation, and make informed financial decisions. Combining the power of ChatGPT with your creativity and expertise, you can unlock a world of opportunities for building sustainable and diverse passive income streams.

Responsible Use of ChatGPT:

It's essential to use ChatGPT responsibly and ethically. While the AI model is a valuable tool, it should not be used to spread misinformation, engage in harmful activities, or perpetuate biased content. Being aware of its limitations and exercising critical judgment when interpreting its responses is crucial to ensure the quality and accuracy of the information it provides.

ChatGPT is here to augment your journey, but it's your ingenuity, dedication, and commitment that will drive your success in the realm of passive income. Let's continue this exciting adventure toward financial freedom, armed with the knowledge of ChatGPT's fundamentals.

Overview of ChatGPT and Its Capabilities

ChatGPT, developed by OpenAI, is a cutting-edge AI language model that belongs to the GPT (Generative Pre-trained Transformer) family. Trained on a massive dataset comprising diverse texts, ChatGPT has an impressive ability to understand and generate human-like text. Its natural language processing (NLP) capabilities enable it to comprehend complex language patterns, context, and semantics, making it an invaluable tool for a wide range of applications.

Language Comprehension:

ChatGPT's primary strength lies in its language comprehension. It can understand and interpret human-generated prompts, questions, and text inputs. By analyzing the context and relationships between words, ChatGPT produces contextually relevant and coherent responses.

Text Generation:

One of the most remarkable capabilities of ChatGPT is its text generation. Given a prompt, it can generate highly realistic and contextually appropriate text. This makes it useful for content creation, writing assistance, and even story generation.

Knowledge Base:

ChatGPT is pre-trained on a vast amount of data up to its knowledge cutoff date in September 2021. As a result, it possesses knowledge spanning numerous subjects, including science, history, technology, literature, and more. Users can tap into this vast knowledge base to gain insights and information.

Creativity and Imagination:

ChatGPT has demonstrated a remarkable capacity for creativity and imagination. It can compose poetry, generate ideas for creative projects, and contribute to storytelling in interactive narratives. This feature makes it a versatile tool for writers, artists, and content creators.

Conversational AI:

ChatGPT excels in engaging in interactive conversations with users. It can maintain context throughout a conversation, answer questions, and respond to prompts in a manner that simulates human-like interaction. Its conversational abilities have made it a popular AI assistant for a variety of applications.

Learning and Adaptation:

While ChatGPT is pre-trained on a vast dataset, it can continue learning and adapting to new information through fine-tuning. This means it can be customized for specific tasks and domains, making it more powerful and relevant in niche applications.

Assistance in Decision Making:

Due to its language comprehension and information synthesis abilities, ChatGPT can assist users in decision-making processes. It can provide insights, suggest strategies, and offer explanations to help users make well-informed choices.

Language Translation:

ChatGPT can assist in language translation tasks, allowing users to input text in one language and receive translations in their desired language. Although not its primary function, it showcases the model's versatility.

It's important to note that while ChatGPT is a powerful tool with numerous capabilities, it also has limitations. It may produce responses that are plausible-sounding but factually incorrect or misleading. Users should exercise critical thinking and verify information obtained through ChatGPT when required.

How ChatGPT learns and improves over time

ChatGPT learns and improves over time through a combination of pre-training and fine-tuning processes. Let's explore each of these stages:

Pre-training:

During the pre-training phase, ChatGPT is exposed to a vast dataset containing a diverse range of texts from the internet. This dataset includes articles, books, websites, and other sources, covering a wide variety of topics up to its knowledge cutoff date in September 2021. The objective of pre-training is to allow the model to learn the statistical patterns, relationships between words, and underlying structures of natural language.

To accomplish this, ChatGPT employs the transformer architecture, a sophisticated deep learning model that excels at capturing long-range dependencies in text. The transformer processes input text in parallel, enabling it to efficiently learn and model complex language patterns.

During pre-training, the model predicts the next word in a sentence given the context of previous words. This process is repeated millions of times across the vast dataset, allowing ChatGPT to gain a deep understanding of language and its nuances.

Fine-tuning:

After the pre-training phase, ChatGPT undergoes fine-tuning, which is a critical step in adapting the model to specific tasks and domains. Fine-tuning involves training the pre-trained model on a narrower dataset, carefully curated for the desired task or application. The fine-tuning dataset includes examples of input text paired with the desired output or a reward signal.

For example, if the goal is to use ChatGPT for customer support, the fine-tuning dataset would consist of conversational data where questions and appropriate responses are provided. During fine-tuning, the model refines its learned representations based on the specific task data and the feedback it receives.

Fine-tuning helps tailor the model's responses to the desired context and improves its performance in the target application. This process enables ChatGPT to become more accurate, contextually aware, and better suited to specific use cases.

User Interaction and Continuous Learning:

In addition to pre-training and fine-tuning, ChatGPT continues to learn and improve over time through user interactions. As users interact with the model, they provide new prompts and queries that the model hasn't encountered during pre-training or fine-tuning.

These interactions contribute to the model's continuous learning process. OpenAI gathers feedback from users and uses this data to periodically update and improve the model. This iterative feedback loop helps address any limitations or errors in ChatGPT's responses, leading to ongoing enhancements and better performance.

It's important to note that while ChatGPT continuously learns and improves, it also relies on the data it was trained on, including both valuable and potentially biased information. OpenAI takes measures to ensure ethical and responsible use of the model, but users should be mindful of its limitations and exercise critical thinking when interpreting its responses.

ChatGPT's ability to learn from vast datasets during pre-training and adapt to specific tasks through fine-tuning, coupled with its ongoing continuous learning from user interactions, enables it to continually evolve and provide increasingly useful and relevant responses to a wide array of queries and prompts.

Real-life applications of ChatGPT in various industries

ChatGPT's versatility and language understanding capabilities have led to its adoption in various industries. Let's explore some real-life applications of ChatGPT across different sectors:

Customer Support:

ChatGPT is employed as a virtual customer support agent in many businesses. It can address customer queries, provide product information, and offer troubleshooting assistance. By handling routine inquiries, ChatGPT frees up human support agents to focus on more complex issues, leading to improved customer satisfaction and cost savings for companies.

Content Creation:

Writers and content creators leverage ChatGPT to generate articles, blog posts, social media content, and product descriptions. ChatGPT's ability to generate coherent and contextually relevant text assists content creators in ideation and production, speeding up the content creation process.

Programming Assistance:

Developers and programmers use ChatGPT to obtain code suggestions and explanations. ChatGPT can help with syntax, logic, and debugging, making it a valuable companion for programmers seeking assistance during software development.

Language Translation:

ChatGPT's language understanding capabilities enable it to aid in language translation tasks. Users can input text in one language and receive translations in their desired language, simplifying communication across linguistic barriers.

Education and Learning:

In the field of education, ChatGPT is utilized to offer explanations, answer questions, and provide study materials for students. It serves as a virtual tutor or educational assistant, helping learners grasp concepts and enhance their understanding of various subjects.

Creative Writing and Storytelling:

Authors and creative writers collaborate with ChatGPT to brainstorm ideas, create fictional characters, and develop engaging narratives. ChatGPT's ability to exhibit creativity and generate text contributes to interactive storytelling and assists writers in overcoming writer's block.

Financial Services:

Financial institutions use ChatGPT to offer personalized financial advice, investment insights, and budgeting tips to their customers. ChatGPT's knowledge of financial markets and products aids users in making informed decisions about their finances.

Healthcare and Medical Support:

In the medical field, ChatGPT has been applied to answer medical queries, provide first aid information, and assist healthcare professionals with quick reference material. It aids in disseminating medical knowledge and offering support to patients.

Human Resources:

HR departments employ ChatGPT for tasks such as answering employee queries, providing onboarding information, and offering HR policy explanations. This helps streamline HR processes and enhances employee experiences.

Virtual Assistants and Smart Devices:

ChatGPT serves as the intelligence behind virtual assistants and smart devices, such as chatbots and voice assistants. It enables natural and interactive communication between users and devices, enhancing user experiences and simplifying daily tasks.

It's important to note that while ChatGPT has numerous applications, its usage should be accompanied by responsible implementation and oversight to ensure ethical and accurate responses. As the technology continues to advance, we can expect even more innovative and impactful applications of ChatGPT across various industries.

3. Leveraging ChatGPT for Content Creation

In this chapter, we will explore how you can harness the power of ChatGPT for content creation and unleash your creativity to produce engaging and valuable content across various platforms.

Ideation and Topic Generation:

One of the biggest challenges in content creation is coming up with fresh and relevant ideas. ChatGPT can be your creative partner, helping you brainstorm ideas for blog posts, articles, social media content, and more. Simply provide a prompt, and ChatGPT will generate a list of potential topics to inspire your content strategy.

Generating Engaging Introductions and Headlines:

The first few sentences and headlines play a crucial role in capturing your audience's attention. ChatGPT can assist in crafting compelling introductions and catchy headlines that pique curiosity and encourage readers to explore your content further.

Outlining and Structuring Content:

A well-organized and coherent structure is vital for content readability. ChatGPT can help you outline your content and suggest appropriate subheadings, ensuring that your ideas flow logically and seamlessly throughout the piece.

Writing Assistance:

Whether you need assistance with fleshing out ideas or overcoming writer's block, ChatGPT is here to lend a helping hand. It can provide additional information, relevant examples, and explanations to support your content and make it more informative and engaging.

Tailoring Content to Your Audience:

Understanding your target audience is crucial for creating content that resonates with them. ChatGPT can analyze your audience demographics and preferences, allowing you to tailor your content to meet their specific needs and interests.

Diversifying Content Formats:

Content creation isn't limited to just text. ChatGPT can assist in generating content across various formats, such as infographics, video scripts, podcast outlines, and more. This versatility enables you to reach a broader audience through different channels.

Enhancing Creativity in Storytelling:

Whether you're crafting fictional narratives or weaving storytelling elements into your content, ChatGPT's creativity can be a valuable asset. It can help you develop characters, devise plot twists, and explore new storytelling angles to captivate your readers.

Language and Style Suggestions:

Consistency in language and style is essential for building your brand voice. ChatGPT can help you maintain a consistent tone and style throughout your content, ensuring that it aligns with your brand identity.

Editing and Revision Support:

After creating your content, ChatGPT can assist in the editing and revision process. It can help spot grammatical errors, improve sentence structures, and suggest enhancements to polish your content before publishing.

Automating Social Media Content:

Managing social media platforms can be time-consuming. ChatGPT can automate social media content creation by generating posts and captions, freeing up your time to focus on other aspects of your content marketing strategy.

Incorporating ChatGPT into your content creation process empowers you to streamline your workflow, spark creativity, and produce high-quality content that resonates with your audience. However, it's essential to maintain a human touch in your content and exercise critical judgment, ensuring that the final output aligns with your brand's values and objectives.

In the next chapter, we'll explore how ChatGPT can be utilized in the realm of online businesses and affiliate marketing to create passive income streams. Get ready to discover exciting possibilities as we dive into the world of e-commerce and digital entrepreneurship.

Using ChatGPT to generate high-quality articles and blog posts

In the fast-paced digital era, content creation is more crucial than ever for businesses and individuals alike. Quality articles and blog posts play a pivotal role in attracting and engaging audiences, establishing authority, and driving traffic to websites. However, crafting compelling and informative content can be a time-consuming task that demands creativity and expertise. Enter ChatGPT, a powerful AI language model that offers a revolutionary solution to streamline and enhance the content creation process.

In this article, we will explore how ChatGPT can be utilized to generate high-quality articles and blog posts, opening up new possibilities for content creators and businesses to excel in the digital landscape.

Understanding ChatGPT's Language Proficiency

ChatGPT's remarkable language proficiency is the foundation of its content generation capabilities. Trained on an extensive dataset comprising diverse texts, ChatGPT has developed a deep understanding of grammar, syntax, and semantics. This enables the model to produce coherent and contextually relevant text, making it an invaluable tool for content creation.

Enhancing Idea Generation and Topic Research

Content creation often begins with brainstorming ideas and conducting topic research. ChatGPT can be an excellent assistant in this regard. By providing a simple prompt or question, content creators can leverage ChatGPT's vast knowledge base to explore various ideas and angles for their articles and blog posts. The model can offer insights into trending topics, keyword suggestions, and relevant subtopics, empowering writers to create content that resonates with their target audience.

Generating Engaging Introductions and Captivating Headlines

Crafting compelling introductions and headlines is vital to grab readers' attention from the outset. ChatGPT can assist in generating attention-grabbing introductions that entice readers to delve further into the content. Moreover, the model's creativity can be harnessed to devise catchy headlines that not only intrigue readers but also optimize search engine discoverability.

Ensuring Coherence and Structure

A well-structured article is key to keeping readers engaged. ChatGPT can help content creators outline and organize their ideas into coherent paragraphs and sections. By suggesting appropriate subheadings and ensuring logical flow, ChatGPT facilitates the creation of articles that are easy to navigate and comprehend.

Tailoring Content to the Target Audience

Understanding the preferences and interests of the target audience is essential for creating relevant and valuable content. ChatGPT's language comprehension allows it to analyze the characteristics of the intended readership. By incorporating this analysis, content creators can tailor their articles and blog posts to meet the specific needs of their audience, leading to increased engagement and loyalty.

Diversifying Content Formats

Content diversity is crucial for reaching a broader audience across various platforms. ChatGPT's versatility enables content creators to explore different content formats such as infographics, listicles, how-to guides, and more. This diversity enriches content offerings and appeals to diverse audience segments.

Optimizing SEO-Friendly Content

Search engine optimization (SEO) is instrumental in improving the visibility and ranking of content on search engines. ChatGPT can be utilized to optimize articles and blog posts by incorporating relevant keywords, meta descriptions, and headers. By adhering to SEO best practices, content creators can increase organic traffic to their websites.

Overcoming Writer's Block and Boosting Productivity

Writer's block is a common challenge faced by content creators. ChatGPT's ability to generate suggestions and ideas can help overcome creative blocks and kickstart the writing process. Moreover, ChatGPT's rapid response time enables writers to maintain their flow of thought and stay productive.

Incorporating Personal Touch and Authenticity

While ChatGPT is a valuable content creation tool, maintaining a personal touch and authenticity is crucial for connecting with readers. Content creators should use ChatGPT's generated text as a foundation and add their unique insights, experiences, and voice to make the content truly their own.

Reviewing and Editing Support

After generating content, it is essential to review and edit the material thoroughly. ChatGPT can be employed to spot grammatical errors, improve sentence structures, and suggest revisions. This editing support streamlines the content refinement process and enhances the overall quality of the final output.

ChatGPT has revolutionized the landscape of content creation by providing an innovative and efficient approach to generating high-quality articles and blog posts. Its language proficiency, idea generation capabilities, and assistance in structuring content empower content creators to reach new heights of creativity and productivity. By leveraging ChatGPT as a collaborative partner, writers can craft engaging, informative, and authentic content that resonates with their audience, thereby amplifying their online presence and influence in the digital world. As AI technology continues to evolve,

ChatGPT holds the promise of transforming content creation and driving meaningful interactions between creators and consumers in the digital age.

Creating engaging social media content with ChatGPT

Social media has emerged as a powerful platform for businesses and individuals to connect with their audience, build brand awareness, and foster meaningful interactions. Engaging social media content is a key driver of success in the digital landscape, as it captures attention, sparks conversations, and encourages audience participation. However, consistently producing captivating content can be challenging, especially with the ever-increasing demand for fresh ideas and creativity. Enter ChatGPT, an advanced AI language model that can be a game-changer in social media content creation. In this article, we will explore how to leverage ChatGPT's capabilities to create engaging and compelling social media content that resonates with your audience and strengthens your online presence.

Ideation and Content Inspiration

One of the first steps in creating compelling social media content is ideation. ChatGPT can be your creative ally, offering a wealth of ideas and inspiration. By providing a simple prompt or topic, ChatGPT can generate diverse content ideas, such as thought-provoking questions, interactive polls, witty captions, and more. This assistance accelerates the content creation process and ensures a steady flow of innovative ideas to keep your social media feeds fresh and engaging.

Crafting Captivating Captions and Introductions

In the fast-paced world of social media, capturing your audience's attention within seconds is crucial. ChatGPT can assist in crafting captivating captions and introductions that entice users to engage with your content further. Whether it's a gripping hook, a call-to-action, or a clever play on words, ChatGPT's language proficiency and creativity can help you stand out in the crowded social media landscape.

Personalization and Audience Connection

Connecting with your audience on a personal level is essential for building brand loyalty and fostering a sense of community. ChatGPT can analyze audience preferences and demographics to help you personalize your content. By tailoring your messaging to suit your target audience's interests and values, you can create a more meaningful and lasting impact on social media.

Visual Content Ideas

Visual content is a driving force in social media engagement. With ChatGPT's assistance, you can generate ideas for eye-catching graphics, infographics, and memes that complement your textual content. By incorporating visually appealing elements, you can make your social media posts more shareable and memorable.

Storytelling and Narrative Building

Storytelling is a potent tool for evoking emotions and creating a lasting impression. ChatGPT's creativity can aid in crafting compelling narratives that resonate with your audience. Whether it's sharing success stories, behind-the-scenes glimpses, or user-generated content, storytelling can foster a sense of authenticity and trust in your brand.

Interactive Content and Polls

Engaging your audience through interactive content and polls is an effective way to increase participation and foster a sense of community. ChatGPT can generate ideas for interactive quizzes, surveys, and polls that encourage user involvement and feedback. Interactive content drives higher engagement rates and provides valuable insights into your audience's preferences.

Hashtag and Trend Suggestions

Keeping up with trending topics and hashtags is crucial for staying relevant on social media. ChatGPT can analyze current trends and suggest relevant hashtags to maximize your content's reach and visibility. Leveraging popular hashtags can also help your content join broader conversations and attract a wider audience.

Cross-Platform Content Adaptation

Each social media platform has its own unique requirements and audience preferences. ChatGPT can assist in adapting your content to suit different platforms while maintaining consistency in messaging and branding. From concise tweets to visually rich Instagram posts, ChatGPT helps you create content tailored to each platform's strengths.

Data-Driven Insights

Analyzing the performance of your social media content is vital for continuous improvement. ChatGPT can help you analyze engagement metrics and derive data-driven insights from your past posts. By identifying successful content patterns and audience behaviors, you can optimize future content strategies for better results.

Scheduling and Post Planning

Efficiently managing your social media content calendar is essential for consistent posting and audience engagement. ChatGPT can assist in scheduling and post planning by generating content in advance. This feature streamlines your workflow and ensures that you stay organized and on top of your content strategy.

In the dynamic world of social media, creating engaging content is crucial for standing out, fostering meaningful connections, and building brand loyalty. With ChatGPT as your creative ally, you gain a powerful tool to streamline the content creation process and generate fresh ideas that resonate with your audience. From crafting captivating captions to incorporating interactive elements, ChatGPT empowers you to create compelling social media content that leaves a lasting impression. As AI technology continues to advance, ChatGPT holds the promise of transforming social media marketing and driving even more impactful interactions between brands and their audience. Embrace the power of ChatGPT, and let your social media content captivate, inspire, and connect with the world.

Monetizing content created by ChatGPT through affiliate marketing and ads

In the digital age, content creation has become a powerful tool for individuals and businesses to share valuable information, connect with audiences, and build online communities. However, creating compelling content is not only about engaging with audiences but also about monetizing the efforts put into content creation. Two popular strategies to monetize content are affiliate marketing and ads. By incorporating these revenue streams into content generated by ChatGPT, content creators can transform their passion into profitable ventures. In this article, we will explore how to effectively monetize content created by ChatGPT through affiliate marketing and ads, providing insights into maximizing returns while maintaining a positive user experience.

Understanding Affiliate Marketing

Affiliate marketing is a performance-based marketing strategy where content creators promote products or services and earn a commission for each sale made through their unique affiliate links. By partnering with relevant affiliate programs, content creators can align their content with products that resonate with their audience's interests and needs.

Identifying Suitable Affiliate Programs

The key to successful affiliate marketing lies in partnering with reputable and relevant affiliate programs. ChatGPT can analyze content topics and suggest affiliate programs that align with the content's theme. For instance, if the content revolves around fitness,

ChatGPT can recommend fitness-related affiliate programs to promote fitness equipment, nutrition supplements, and workout plans.

Crafting Persuasive Product Recommendations

Generating high-quality and persuasive product recommendations is essential to entice audiences to click on affiliate links and make purchases. ChatGPT can assist in crafting persuasive and informative product reviews, comparisons, and buying guides that address the audience's pain points and encourage informed buying decisions.

Strategic Placement of Affiliate Links

Strategic placement of affiliate links is crucial to optimize click-through rates and conversions. ChatGPT can suggest suitable spots within the content where affiliate links can be seamlessly integrated without disrupting the user experience. Balancing the promotion of affiliate products with valuable content is vital to maintain trust with the audience.

Analyzing Affiliate Performance Metrics

Tracking the performance of affiliate marketing efforts is critical to evaluate the effectiveness of campaigns and optimize strategies. ChatGPT can analyze affiliate performance metrics, such as click-through rates, conversion rates, and revenue generated. These insights enable content creators to refine their approach and focus on promoting products that yield higher returns.

Leveraging Display Ads

In addition to affiliate marketing, content creators can monetize content through display ads. Display ads are graphical or text-based advertisements that appear within the content or on the website. ChatGPT can assist in identifying suitable ad networks and ad placements to maximize ad revenue while maintaining a user-friendly browsing experience.

Implementing Responsive Ad Formats

With users accessing content through various devices, it's essential to implement responsive ad formats that adapt to different screen sizes. ChatGPT can suggest responsive ad units that ensure ads display optimally on desktops, mobile devices, and tablets, enhancing user engagement and ad performance.

Balancing User Experience and Monetization

Maintaining a positive user experience is crucial for audience retention and engagement. ChatGPT can help content creators strike a balance between monetization efforts and user experience by suggesting ad frequency and placement strategies that do not overwhelm the audience.

Experimenting with A/B Testing

A/B testing is a valuable tool to optimize ad performance and maximize revenue. By experimenting with different ad formats, sizes, and placements, content creators can use ChatGPT to analyze and identify the most effective ad configurations for their audience.

Diversifying Revenue Streams

Diversifying revenue streams is essential for long-term sustainability. ChatGPT can recommend additional monetization strategies, such as sponsored content, premium subscriptions, or digital product sales. This diversification helps content creators reduce reliance on a single revenue source and provides more stability to their income.

Monetizing content created by ChatGPT through affiliate marketing and ads offers content creators an opportunity to transform their passion into profitable ventures. By leveraging ChatGPT's language proficiency and insights, content creators can identify suitable affiliate programs, craft persuasive product recommendations, and strategically implement ads to maximize revenue. Balancing monetization efforts with user experience is essential for maintaining audience trust and engagement. Diversifying revenue streams provides additional stability and long-term viability. As AI technology continues to evolve, ChatGPT holds the promise of being a valuable partner in content monetization, empowering creators to turn their content into a lucrative business while maintaining a positive impact on their audience. By embracing the potential of ChatGPT, content creators can pave the way toward a sustainable and prosperous future in the ever-evolving digital landscape.

4. Building Niche Websites with ChatGPT

Niche websites serve as focused platforms that cater to specific audiences with a shared interest or passion. These websites are an excellent way to establish authority, connect with like-minded individuals, and monetize content in targeted markets. With the assistance of ChatGPT, content creation and optimization for niche websites can be streamlined, allowing creators to create valuable and engaging content. In this chapter, we will explore how to build niche websites with ChatGPT, leveraging its language proficiency and insights to create a compelling online presence.

Identifying Lucrative Niche Markets

The foundation of a successful niche website lies in identifying lucrative and underserved niche markets. ChatGPT can assist in researching and analyzing potential niches by evaluating search volume, competition, and audience demand. This analysis ensures that the chosen niche has sufficient potential for growth and profitability.

Generating Keyword-Rich Content

Keyword research is critical for niche website success as it helps in attracting organic traffic. ChatGPT can analyze keywords and provide content ideas centered around relevant and high-ranking keywords. By generating keyword-rich content, niche websites can optimize their chances of ranking higher in search engine results.

Crafting Comprehensive Niche Guides

Creating comprehensive niche guides that cover specific topics in-depth can establish a niche website's authority. ChatGPT can assist in crafting detailed and informative guides that address the audience's pain points and provide valuable insights. These guides can position the website as a go-to resource for niche-related information.

Leveraging ChatGPT for Content Ideation

Content ideation is a continuous process that requires fresh ideas and creativity. ChatGPT can be used to brainstorm content ideas, generate blog post titles, and offer unique angles to explore within the chosen niche. This collaboration ensures a steady flow of content that keeps the audience engaged.

Curating User-Generated Content

Engaging with the niche community and curating user-generated content can foster a sense of community and authenticity. ChatGPT can help in identifying relevant user-generated content and strategizing how to incorporate it into the website. This interactive approach strengthens the website's relationship with its audience.

Personalizing User Experience

Personalization is crucial for niche websites to cater to the specific needs and interests of their audience. ChatGPT can analyze user behavior and preferences to suggest personalized content recommendations and user experiences. This level of personalization enhances user engagement and satisfaction.

Monetization Strategies for Niche Websites

Monetizing niche websites can be achieved through various strategies, such as affiliate marketing, display ads, sponsored content, and digital products. ChatGPT can analyze the niche market and recommend the most suitable monetization methods based on the website's goals and audience preferences.

Optimizing Website Structure and Navigation

A well-organized website structure and intuitive navigation are essential for user experience and search engine optimization. ChatGPT can assist in suggesting the optimal website layout and navigation to enhance user engagement and site visibility.

Analyzing Website Performance Metrics

Monitoring website performance metrics is crucial for understanding user behavior and making data-driven decisions. ChatGPT can analyze website analytics and provide insights into traffic sources, user engagement, and conversion rates. These insights enable website owners to refine their strategies for continuous improvement.

Staying Updated with Niche Trends

Niche markets are dynamic and can experience rapid changes. ChatGPT can help content creators stay updated with niche trends and industry developments. By monitoring industry news and analyzing relevant data, niche websites can adapt their content strategy to remain relevant and authoritative.

Building niche websites with ChatGPT offers content creators a powerful ally in establishing authoritative and profitable platforms. By identifying lucrative niche markets, generating keyword-rich content, and crafting comprehensive guides, niche websites can attract targeted audiences and generate organic traffic. Leveraging ChatGPT for content ideation, user experience personalization, and website performance analysis enhances the website's impact and engagement. Effective monetization strategies, guided by ChatGPT's insights, ensure long-term sustainability and profitability. By staying updated with niche trends and continuously optimizing the website, content creators can build thriving niche websites that resonate with their audience, establish authority, and open new avenues for success. With the synergy of ChatGPT and niche website creation, creators can carve their niche in the digital landscape and foster a thriving online community.

Identifying profitable niches for websites

Identifying profitable niches for websites is a critical step in building a successful online platform. Choosing the right niche ensures that the website caters to a specific target audience, has potential for growth, and offers opportunities for monetization. Here are some strategies to help identify profitable niches for websites:

Passion and Interest:

Start by considering your own passions and interests. Building a website around a topic that genuinely excites you can keep you motivated and engaged in the long run. Your passion will reflect in your content and resonate with like-minded individuals, creating a dedicated audience.

Market Research:

Conduct thorough market research to identify gaps and opportunities in the market. Look for niche areas where there is demand but limited competition. Tools like Google Trends, keyword research tools, and competitor analysis can provide valuable insights into popular topics and search trends.

Audience Demand:

Consider the needs and interests of your target audience. Are there specific problems they are trying to solve or topics they are eager to learn about? Identifying audience demand ensures that your website addresses real-world challenges and attracts a committed audience.

Long-Tail Keywords:

Explore long-tail keywords related to potential niches. Long-tail keywords are more specific and can indicate highly targeted search intent. They may have lower search volume, but they often lead to higher conversion rates due to their relevance.

Profitability and Monetization:

Assess the monetization potential of the niche. Consider how you can generate revenue through affiliate marketing, display ads, sponsored content, or selling digital products. A profitable niche is one where there are viable monetization options.

Trends and Evergreen Topics:

Balance trending topics with evergreen content. While trending topics can attract immediate attention, evergreen content remains relevant over time, ensuring a steady flow of traffic to your website.

Target Audience Size:

Evaluate the size of your target audience. A niche with a sizable and engaged audience is more likely to offer long-term growth and profitability.

Problem Solving:

Look for niches where you can provide solutions or valuable information. Websites that address specific problems or offer practical advice tend to attract loyal followers.

Passionate Communities:

Explore online forums, social media groups, and other platforms to find passionate communities discussing specific topics. Engaged communities indicate a strong interest in the niche and potential for audience building.

Uniqueness and Differentiation:

Consider how you can bring a unique perspective or approach to the niche. Differentiating your website from others in the same niche helps you stand out and attract a dedicated following.

Identifying profitable niches for websites requires a combination of passion, research, and understanding of audience needs. By focusing on topics that align with your interests, cater to audience demand, and offer opportunities for monetization, you can build a successful website that resonates with your target audience and provides value in the digital landscape. Through strategic niche selection and effective content creation, you can create a thriving online platform that generates both engagement and revenue.

Setting up niche websites and integrating ChatGPT

Setting up niche websites and integrating ChatGPT can be a powerful combination to create engaging and valuable online platforms. By leveraging the benefits of niche-focused content and the language proficiency of ChatGPT, you can provide personalized and relevant experiences for your target audience. Let's explore the steps to set up niche websites and integrate ChatGPT effectively:

Choose a Profitable Niche:

Select a niche that aligns with your interests and has the potential for profitability. Conduct thorough market research to identify audience demand, competition, and monetization opportunities within the chosen niche.

Domain and Hosting:

Register a domain name that reflects your niche and is easy to remember. Choose a reliable web hosting provider that ensures fast loading times and minimal downtime for your website.

Design and User Experience:

Create a visually appealing and user-friendly website design. Focus on providing easy navigation and intuitive layout to enhance the user experience. Ensure that your website is mobile-responsive for users on various devices.

Keyword Research:

Conduct keyword research to identify relevant and high-ranking keywords within your niche. Use these keywords strategically in your content to improve search engine visibility and attract organic traffic.

Content Strategy:

Develop a content strategy that caters to your target audience's interests and needs. Plan a mix of evergreen and trending content to maintain relevance and steady traffic flow. Integrate ChatGPT into your content creation process to generate fresh and engaging ideas.

ChatGPT Integration:

Choose a suitable integration method for ChatGPT on your website. You can use the OpenAI API to interact with ChatGPT and generate responses based on user prompts. Integrate ChatGPT into your website's chatbot, contact forms, or interactive elements to offer personalized interactions with your audience.

Customizing ChatGPT Responses:

Customize ChatGPT responses to align with your website's tone and branding. Ensure that the language generated by ChatGPT is consistent with your niche's subject matter and provides valuable insights to users.

Engaging User Experience:

Leverage ChatGPT to offer interactive and engaging user experiences. Create quizzes, polls, or personalized content recommendations using ChatGPT to encourage user participation and increase time spent on your website.

Optimize for Performance:

Regularly monitor your website's performance and user engagement metrics. Use analytics to gain insights into user behavior, popular content, and areas for improvement. Optimize your website and ChatGPT interactions based on this data.

Stay Updated and Evolve:

Keep your website and content updated with the latest trends and developments within your niche. Evolve your ChatGPT interactions based on user feedback and changing audience preferences.

Building niche websites and integrating ChatGPT is a dynamic process that involves strategic planning, content creation, and user engagement. By focusing on a profitable niche and providing valuable content tailored to your target audience, you can attract and retain a dedicated following. ChatGPT integration enhances the user experience by offering personalized interactions and fresh content ideas. As you continuously optimize your website and ChatGPT interactions, you can create a thriving online platform that establishes authority in your niche and fosters meaningful connections with your audience. The synergy of niche-focused content and AI-driven language capabilities empowers you to make a significant impact in the digital landscape.

Driving traffic and monetizing niche websites for passive income

Driving traffic and effectively monetizing niche websites are key strategies to generate passive income. By attracting a steady flow of targeted visitors and implementing diverse monetization methods, you can turn your niche website into a lucrative source of passive revenue. Let's explore the steps to drive traffic and monetize your niche website for passive income:

Search Engine Optimization (SEO):

Optimize your website for search engines to improve its visibility in organic search results. Conduct keyword research and incorporate relevant keywords into your content. Create high-quality, valuable content that addresses your audience's needs and interests, making your website more appealing to search engines and users.

Content Marketing:

Utilize content marketing to attract and engage your target audience. Create blog posts, articles, videos, infographics, and other valuable content that showcases your expertise in the niche. Share your content on social media platforms and relevant online communities to increase visibility and drive traffic.

Email Marketing:

Build an email list of interested subscribers and regularly send them updates, newsletters, and exclusive content related to your niche. Email marketing is a powerful way to nurture relationships with your audience, promote your website's content, and drive traffic back to your website.

Social Media Marketing:

Leverage social media platforms to promote your niche website and engage with your audience. Share your content, interact with followers, participate in relevant discussions, and use social media advertising to reach a broader audience.

Guest Blogging and Backlinks:

Collaborate with other websites and blogs in your niche through guest blogging. By providing valuable content on other platforms, you can reach new audiences and build backlinks to your website, which boosts its search engine ranking and traffic.

Community Engagement:

Actively engage with your niche community by participating in forums, social media groups, and online communities. Offer valuable insights, answer questions, and contribute to discussions. Being an active and helpful member of the community establishes your authority and drives traffic to your website.

Optimize Website Performance:

Ensure that your website loads quickly and is mobile-responsive. A fast and user-friendly website enhances user experience and encourages visitors to explore more of your content.

Monetization Methods:

Implement various monetization methods on your niche website to generate passive income. Some popular options include:

a. Affiliate Marketing: Promote products or services related to your niche and earn commissions for every sale made through your affiliate links.

b. Display Ads: Place relevant display ads on your website and earn revenue based on ad impressions and clicks.

c. Sponsored Content: Collaborate with brands or companies in your niche to publish sponsored posts or reviews for compensation.

d. Digital Products: Create and sell digital products such as eBooks, online courses, templates, or software related to your niche.

Test and Optimize:

Continuously test different monetization methods and website strategies to determine what works best for your niche and audience. Analyze website performance metrics and user behavior to optimize your website and monetization efforts for maximum returns.

Diversify Income Streams:

To create a more stable and diversified passive income, consider expanding your website's revenue streams. Explore additional opportunities, such as membership subscriptions, premium content, or offering consulting services within your niche.

Driving traffic and monetizing niche websites for passive income require a combination of effective marketing strategies and well-implemented monetization methods. By focusing on delivering valuable content, engaging with your audience, and diversifying your income streams, you can build a successful niche website that generates sustainable passive income. Stay committed to continuous improvement, and leverage data-driven insights to optimize your website and monetization efforts for long-term success. With dedication and strategic planning, your niche website can become a reliable source of passive income, allowing you to enjoy financial freedom and pursue your passions.

5. ChatGPT and the World of E-commerce

The world of e-commerce has undergone significant transformations in recent years, with consumer preferences shifting towards online shopping and personalized experiences. In this digital era, ChatGPT plays a crucial role in enhancing the e-commerce landscape by providing personalized recommendations, addressing customer queries, and streamlining customer interactions. In this chapter, we will explore how ChatGPT is revolutionizing the world of e-commerce and revolutionizing the way businesses connect with their customers.

Personalized Product Recommendations

One of the most significant advantages of integrating ChatGPT into e-commerce platforms is the ability to offer personalized product recommendations. By analyzing customer behavior, preferences, and purchase history, ChatGPT can suggest relevant products tailored to each individual, increasing the likelihood of conversion and enhancing the overall shopping experience.

Chatbots for Customer Support

Chatbots powered by ChatGPT have transformed customer support in the e-commerce industry. These AI-driven assistants are available 24/7 to address customer queries, resolve issues, and provide real-time assistance. With ChatGPT's natural language processing capabilities, chatbots can understand and respond to customer inquiries in a human-like manner, leading to improved customer satisfaction.

Improved User Engagement

Engaging users and keeping them on the website is vital for e-commerce success. ChatGPT helps e-commerce businesses achieve this by offering interactive elements such as quizzes, polls, and personalized content. Engaged users are more likely to spend more time on the website, explore product offerings, and make repeat purchases.

Virtual Shopping Assistants

In the absence of physical sales assistants, virtual shopping assistants powered by ChatGPT step in to provide guidance and support during the shopping process. These assistants can help customers find the right products, provide size and fit recommendations, and offer styling suggestions, creating a personalized and interactive shopping experience.

Enhanced Product Descriptions

Creating compelling product descriptions is crucial for e-commerce success. ChatGPT can assist in generating product descriptions that are informative, engaging, and optimized for search engines. Improved product descriptions can boost search visibility and attract more potential customers to the website.

Natural Language Search

E-commerce search functionality has advanced significantly with the integration of ChatGPT's natural language processing capabilities. Customers can use conversational queries to find specific products, making the search process more intuitive and efficient.

Abandoned Cart Recovery

Cart abandonment is a common challenge for e-commerce businesses. ChatGPT-powered systems can engage with customers who have abandoned their carts, offering incentives, discounts, or personalized recommendations to encourage them to complete their purchases.

Inventory Management and Order Tracking

ChatGPT can also streamline inventory management and order tracking processes. Customers can inquire about product availability, shipping updates, and order statuses through chatbots, reducing the burden on customer support teams.

Upselling and Cross-selling Opportunities

Intelligent upselling and cross-selling strategies can boost revenue for e-commerce businesses. ChatGPT can analyze customer behavior and recommend complementary or upgraded products during the shopping journey, increasing the average order value.

Customer Feedback and Reviews

ChatGPT can also play a role in gathering customer feedback and generating product reviews. By engaging customers post-purchase, e-commerce businesses can improve their offerings based on customer insights and build trust among potential buyers.

ChatGPT's integration into the world of e-commerce has transformed the way businesses connect with their customers and enhance the online shopping experience. From personalized product recommendations to virtual shopping assistants, ChatGPT's language proficiency and natural language processing capabilities have revolutionized various aspects of e-commerce operations. By leveraging ChatGPT, e-commerce businesses can provide more personalized, interactive, and efficient services, driving customer satisfaction and loyalty. As AI technology continues to evolve, ChatGPT holds the potential to shape the future of e-commerce, paving the way for more personalized and engaging shopping experiences for customers worldwide. Embracing ChatGPT's capabilities in e-commerce can give businesses a competitive edge and position them for success in the ever-evolving digital marketplace.

Utilizing ChatGPT for product descriptions and reviews

Utilizing ChatGPT for product descriptions and reviews can significantly enhance the quality and efficiency of content creation for e-commerce businesses. By leveraging ChatGPT's language proficiency and natural language generation capabilities, product descriptions can be made more engaging and informative, while reviews can be generated to provide valuable insights for potential customers. Let's explore how ChatGPT can be effectively used for product descriptions and reviews:

Engaging Product Descriptions:

ChatGPT can be employed to generate compelling and engaging product descriptions. By providing relevant information about the product, its features, benefits, and use cases, ChatGPT can help businesses create detailed and persuasive descriptions that entice potential customers to make a purchase.

Personalized Descriptions:

Using ChatGPT, businesses can tailor product descriptions based on customer preferences and behavior. By analyzing customer data and purchase history, ChatGPT can generate personalized product descriptions that address individual needs and interests, leading to higher engagement and conversion rates.

SEO-Optimized Content:

ChatGPT can be used to create product descriptions that are optimized for search engines. By incorporating relevant keywords and search terms, businesses can improve the visibility of their products in online searches, driving organic traffic to their e-commerce websites.

Product Comparison:

ChatGPT can assist in creating product comparison content. By analyzing the specifications and features of different products, ChatGPT can generate informative comparisons that help customers make informed decisions.

Generating Product Reviews:

Customer reviews play a pivotal role in influencing purchase decisions. ChatGPT can be utilized to generate product reviews based on customer feedback and sentiments. These reviews can provide valuable insights to potential buyers, building trust and credibility for the product.

Real-Time Review Analysis:

ChatGPT-powered systems can analyze customer reviews in real-time to identify patterns, sentiments, and common concerns. This analysis can help businesses make data-driven decisions to improve their products and services.

Response to Customer Queries:

Incorporating ChatGPT into the review section can allow businesses to respond to customer queries and concerns promptly. Automated responses can address common questions, enhancing customer support and satisfaction.

Generating User-Generated Content:

ChatGPT can encourage user-generated content by prompting customers to share their experiences and opinions. By utilizing ChatGPT to engage customers in conversation, businesses can gather valuable user-generated content for reviews.

Multilingual Capabilities:

ChatGPT's multilingual capabilities enable businesses to provide product descriptions and reviews in different languages, catering to a broader international audience.

Customization for Brand Voice:

Businesses can customize ChatGPT's language generation to match their brand voice and tone. This ensures that product descriptions and reviews align with the overall branding strategy.

Integrating ChatGPT into e-commerce operations for product descriptions and reviews offers businesses a powerful tool to create engaging, informative, and personalized content. By leveraging ChatGPT's language proficiency and natural language generation capabilities, businesses can enhance customer engagement, improve search engine visibility, and build trust among potential buyers. The versatility of ChatGPT in generating multilingual content and responding to customer queries contributes to a seamless and customer-centric shopping experience. By utilizing ChatGPT's capabilities in product descriptions and reviews, businesses can stay ahead of the competition and create a lasting impact on their target audience in the highly competitive e-commerce landscape.

Implementing ChatGPT-driven chatbots for customer support

Implementing ChatGPT-driven chatbots for customer support is an excellent way to provide efficient and responsive assistance to customers. These AI-powered chatbots can handle a wide range of customer inquiries, address common issues, and offer real-time support, freeing up human agents to focus on more complex tasks. Here's a step-by-step guide on how to implement ChatGPT-driven chatbots for customer support:

Define the Scope and Goals:

Start by defining the scope of your chatbot's capabilities and the specific goals you want to achieve with it. Determine the types of customer inquiries the chatbot will handle, such as product questions, order status inquiries, and general FAQs.

Choose a Chatbot Platform:

Select a suitable chatbot platform or framework that supports the integration of ChatGPT. There are various AI chatbot platforms available, some of which offer pre-built chatbot templates that you can customize for your specific needs.

Train the Chatbot with ChatGPT:

Train the chatbot using ChatGPT to understand customer queries and generate relevant responses. Fine-tune the language model to ensure that the chatbot provides accurate and contextually appropriate answers.

Build Conversation Flows:

Create conversation flows that guide the interaction between the chatbot and customers. Design a logical and intuitive conversation path to handle different types of inquiries effectively.

Integrate with Customer Support Channels:

Integrate the chatbot with your customer support channels, such as your website, mobile app, or social media platforms. Ensure a seamless user experience by making the chatbot easily accessible to customers.

Test and Optimize:

Thoroughly test the chatbot to identify any potential issues or areas for improvement. Collect feedback from customers and use it to optimize the chatbot's responses and improve its performance.

Implement Natural Language Processing (NLP):

Incorporate natural language processing (NLP) capabilities into the chatbot to understand the nuances of customer queries. NLP enables the chatbot to handle variations in phrasing and deliver more human-like responses.

Offer Escalation Options:

Include escalation options in the chatbot's conversation flow. If the chatbot cannot resolve a complex issue, it should smoothly transfer the conversation to a human customer support agent for further assistance.

Regularly Update and Improve:

Regularly update the chatbot's knowledge base with new information, product updates, and frequently asked questions. Continuous improvement ensures that the chatbot stays relevant and effective in addressing customer inquiries.

Monitor Performance Metrics:

Monitor key performance metrics, such as customer satisfaction, response time, and issue resolution rate. Use these metrics to evaluate the chatbot's effectiveness and make data-driven decisions for improvement.

Implementing ChatGPT-driven chatbots for customer support can significantly enhance the efficiency and effectiveness of your customer service operations. By leveraging ChatGPT's language proficiency and natural language processing capabilities, you can provide prompt and accurate responses to customer inquiries, improve customer satisfaction, and optimize your customer support processes. As AI technology continues to advance, ChatGPT-driven chatbots offer businesses a valuable tool to deliver exceptional customer experiences and streamline their customer support operations. Embrace the potential of ChatGPT-driven chatbots, and empower your business to excel in the ever-evolving landscape of customer support.

Increasing e-commerce sales using AI-powered recommendations

In the rapidly evolving world of e-commerce, staying ahead of the competition and increasing sales requires innovative strategies that resonate with customers. One of the most powerful tools at the disposal of e-commerce businesses is AI-powered recommendations. By leveraging artificial intelligence and machine learning algorithms, businesses can deliver personalized product recommendations that cater to the unique preferences and needs of each customer.

Personalized Product Recommendations:

AI-powered recommendation engines analyze vast amounts of customer data, including browsing history, purchase behavior, and preferences, to generate personalized product recommendations. By offering customers products that align with their interests, businesses can increase the chances of conversion and drive sales.

Understanding Customer Behavior:

AI-powered recommendation systems are designed to understand customer behavior and buying patterns. By gaining insights into customer preferences and purchase history, businesses can anticipate customer needs and present relevant products at the right time, fostering a sense of understanding and connection with the customer.

Cross-Selling and Upselling Opportunities:

AI-powered recommendation engines can identify cross-selling and upselling opportunities by suggesting complementary or higher-priced products based on the customer's current selection. This approach not only increases the average order value but also enhances the customer's overall shopping experience.

Real-Time Personalization:

AI-powered recommendation systems can provide real-time personalization, dynamically adjusting recommendations as customers browse the website. By continuously updating recommendations based on customer interactions, businesses can engage customers throughout their shopping journey and encourage impulse purchases.

Improving User Engagement:

Personalized product recommendations create a more engaging and enjoyable shopping experience. Customers are more likely to spend time exploring relevant products, leading to increased session duration and higher chances of finding products that resonate with their interests.

Reducing Decision Fatigue:

The vast product offerings on e-commerce websites can lead to decision fatigue for customers. AI-powered recommendations simplify the decision-making process by presenting customers with a curated selection of products, making it easier for them to find what they are looking for.

Email and Retargeting Campaigns:

AI-powered recommendation systems can be integrated into email marketing and retargeting campaigns. By tailoring email recommendations to each customer's preferences, businesses can increase email open rates, click-through rates, and conversion rates.

Segment-Specific Recommendations:

AI-powered recommendation engines can provide segment-specific recommendations based on customer demographics, behavior, and location. This level of customization allows businesses to target different customer segments with relevant product offerings, optimizing marketing efforts.

A/B Testing and Optimization:

AI-powered recommendation systems can facilitate A/B testing of different recommendation algorithms and strategies. By analyzing the performance of various recommendation models, businesses can fine-tune their approach to maximize sales.

Continuous Learning and Improvement:

AI-powered recommendation engines continuously learn from customer interactions and feedback. As the system accumulates more data, its recommendations become increasingly accurate and tailored to individual customer preferences, creating a virtuous cycle of improvement.

AI-powered recommendations have become a game-changer for e-commerce businesses seeking to increase sales and enhance customer satisfaction. By delivering personalized product recommendations, understanding customer behavior, and offering real-time personalization, businesses can create a seamless and delightful shopping experience. AI-powered recommendation engines not only boost sales but also foster customer loyalty and engagement, positioning businesses for long-term success in the highly competitive e-commerce landscape. As technology continues to advance, the role of AI in e-commerce will continue to grow, and businesses that embrace AI-powered recommendations will gain a significant competitive advantage in the digital marketplace.

The chapter highlights various applications of ChatGPT in the e-commerce landscape:

Personalized Product Recommendations: ChatGPT enables businesses to offer personalized product recommendations by analyzing customer behavior, preferences, and purchase history. This level of personalization enhances customer engagement and increases the likelihood of conversion.

Chatbots for Customer Support: AI-powered chatbots driven by ChatGPT serve as virtual assistants, providing 24/7 customer support. These chatbots can respond to inquiries in a human-like manner, resolve common issues, and free up human agents for more complex tasks.

Improved User Engagement: By integrating ChatGPT, e-commerce businesses can engage users through interactive elements like quizzes, polls, and personalized content. Engaged users are more likely to spend time on the website and explore product offerings.

Virtual Shopping Assistants: ChatGPT-driven virtual shopping assistants guide customers through the shopping process, providing personalized recommendations, size and fit advice, and styling suggestions.

Enhanced Product Descriptions: Businesses can leverage ChatGPT to generate informative and SEO-optimized product descriptions, improving search engine visibility and attracting potential customers.

Natural Language Search: ChatGPT's natural language processing capabilities enable e-commerce platforms to understand conversational queries, making the search process more intuitive and efficient.

Abandoned Cart Recovery: ChatGPT-powered systems can engage customers who abandon their carts, offering incentives and personalized recommendations to encourage them to complete their purchases.

Real-Time Review Analysis: ChatGPT can analyze customer reviews in real-time, providing valuable insights to businesses for improving their products and services.

The chapter emphasizes the role of ChatGPT in personalization, efficiency, and customer-centricity, leading to enhanced customer experiences and increased sales in the e-commerce industry. It also highlights the importance of continuous improvement and data-driven decision-making to optimize the integration of ChatGPT in e-commerce operations.

By embracing ChatGPT's capabilities, e-commerce businesses can gain a competitive edge, foster customer loyalty, and create a lasting impact in the dynamic and ever-evolving landscape of online retail.

6. ChatGPT in Investment and Trading

The world of investment and trading is characterized by its dynamic nature, where timely decision-making and access to relevant information are crucial for success. In recent years, artificial intelligence has made significant strides in transforming this landscape, and ChatGPT emerges as a powerful tool for investors and traders alike. In this chapter, we will explore how ChatGPT is revolutionizing investment and trading practices, providing valuable insights, and assisting users in making more informed and data-driven decisions.

Sentiment Analysis and Market Trends

ChatGPT's natural language processing capabilities enable it to analyze vast amounts of financial news, social media posts, and market data to gauge market sentiment and trends. By interpreting sentiment, investors and traders can better understand the overall market sentiment, potential risks, and opportunities for profit.

Real-Time Financial News Updates

Keeping track of real-time financial news and developments is essential in investment and trading. ChatGPT can provide instant updates on breaking news, earnings reports, economic indicators, and geopolitical events that may impact financial markets. This timely information empowers users to make well-informed decisions.

Technical Analysis and Charting

ChatGPT can assist in technical analysis by generating insights from price charts and historical market data. Traders can receive trend analysis, pattern recognition, and support/resistance levels, enhancing their understanding of market movements and potential entry and exit points.

Algorithmic Trading Strategies

Leveraging ChatGPT, traders can create and optimize algorithmic trading strategies. By analyzing historical market data and patterns, ChatGPT can suggest potential trading algorithms that traders can backtest and implement for automated trading.

Risk Assessment and Portfolio Management

Risk management is crucial in investment and trading. ChatGPT can assess portfolio risk by analyzing asset correlations, volatility, and market conditions. Investors can adjust their portfolio allocation based on ChatGPT's insights to achieve better risk-adjusted returns.

Market Sentiment-Driven Trading

ChatGPT can provide valuable sentiment-driven trading signals. By analyzing social media and news sentiment, traders can make decisions based on market sentiment and quickly adapt to changing market dynamics.

Financial Education and Learning Resources

ChatGPT can act as a personalized financial education tool, offering insights and explanations of complex financial concepts to users. Novice investors and traders can benefit from ChatGPT's guidance and learn at their own pace.

Simulated Trading and Backtesting

Investors and traders can use ChatGPT to simulate trading strategies and backtest them using historical market data. This allows users to evaluate the performance of their strategies and refine them before deploying real capital.

Market Monitoring and Alerts

ChatGPT can monitor financial markets and notify users of significant events, price movements, or specific market conditions through real-time alerts. Traders can stay informed and respond promptly to potential trading opportunities.

Portfolio Optimization and Diversification

By analyzing historical data and asset correlations, ChatGPT can assist investors in optimizing their portfolios and suggesting diversified asset allocations. Diversification helps reduce risk and enhance long-term portfolio performance.

ChatGPT's integration into investment and trading practices has introduced a new paradigm, empowering investors and traders with powerful AI-driven insights and support. By leveraging natural language processing, sentiment analysis, and technical analysis, ChatGPT enables more informed decision-making and improves risk management in financial markets. The real-time financial news updates and market monitoring capabilities keep users well-informed of critical events and market trends.

For traders, ChatGPT opens the door to algorithmic trading and technical analysis, allowing for more systematic and data-driven strategies. Investors can benefit from ChatGPT's portfolio optimization suggestions, aiding in building well-diversified portfolios that align with their risk tolerance and financial goals.

ChatGPT serves as a valuable educational resource for financial literacy, making complex financial concepts accessible and understandable to all levels of investors and traders.

As AI technology continues to evolve, the potential of ChatGPT in investment and trading will only expand, enabling users to navigate financial markets with greater confidence and efficiency. The combination of human expertise and AI-driven insights paves the way for a more inclusive and informed investment and trading landscape. Embracing ChatGPT's capabilities offers investors and traders a competitive edge in the fast-paced and ever-changing world of finance.

The integration of ChatGPT in investment and trading practices has the potential to democratize access to financial markets. Historically, the world of finance has been dominated by institutional investors and sophisticated trading firms with access to advanced analytics and data. However, ChatGPT's user-friendly interface and accessibility make it a valuable tool for individual investors and retail traders, leveling the playing field and enabling them to make more informed decisions.

For novice investors, ChatGPT serves as a valuable mentor, guiding them through the complexities of financial markets. Its ability to provide explanations of financial concepts in plain language fosters financial education and empowers individuals to take control of their investments. With ChatGPT's insights at their disposal, investors can gain confidence in their decision-making and gradually develop their investment acumen.

Institutional investors and professional traders can also benefit from ChatGPT's analytical capabilities. By complementing their own research and expertise with AI-driven insights, they can validate their strategies, discover new opportunities, and enhance their risk management practices.

Moreover, the implementation of AI-driven algorithms and automated trading strategies based on ChatGPT's recommendations has the potential to improve market efficiency. These algorithms can quickly respond to market signals, leading to more liquid and stable markets. However, it is essential to ensure that these algorithms are well-designed and tested to prevent unintended consequences and market disruptions.

As with any AI-powered tool, it is crucial to exercise caution and not solely rely on ChatGPT's recommendations. The human touch and intuition in investment and trading decisions remain invaluable. ChatGPT should be seen as a powerful enhancement to traditional methods, offering data-driven insights and augmenting human expertise, rather than a replacement for human decision-making.

It is also essential to acknowledge that the financial markets are inherently unpredictable and subject to various external factors, including economic conditions, geopolitical events, and technological advancements. While ChatGPT can provide valuable analysis and insights, it cannot predict the future with certainty. Investors and traders must always approach the markets with a long-term perspective, discipline, and risk management practices.

Security and data privacy are critical considerations when implementing ChatGPT in investment and trading processes. AI systems must be protected from potential vulnerabilities and unauthorized access. Additionally, users' sensitive financial information should be handled with utmost care to maintain confidentiality and trust.

In conclusion, ChatGPT's integration into investment and trading practices marks a significant milestone in the evolution of the financial industry. Its natural language processing and analytical capabilities offer valuable insights, real-time updates, and personalized guidance to investors and traders. By empowering individuals with AI-driven knowledge and recommendations, ChatGPT contributes to a more informed, inclusive, and data-driven investment landscape.

As AI technology continues to advance, the potential of ChatGPT in finance is likely to expand, enabling further innovation and optimization in investment and trading strategies. Investors, traders, and financial institutions must embrace AI responsibly, using it as a powerful tool to augment their decision-making processes and navigate the complexities of financial markets successfully.

Ultimately, the harmonious collaboration between human expertise and AI-driven insights will pave the way for a more efficient, transparent, and prosperous financial ecosystem, benefiting all participants and contributing to a more sustainable and resilient global economy.

Understanding AI's role in investment decisions

AI plays a transformative role in investment decisions, revolutionizing the way investment professionals and individuals analyze financial markets, identify opportunities, and manage risk. AI-powered tools, such as machine learning algorithms and natural language processing, have the capacity to process vast amounts of data and extract valuable insights, leading to more informed and data-driven investment strategies. Here are some key aspects of AI's role in investment decisions:

Data Analysis and Pattern Recognition:

AI excels at analyzing large datasets, historical market data, economic indicators, and news events. Machine learning algorithms can identify patterns and trends that may be challenging for human investors to detect. This helps investors make more informed decisions based on data-driven insights.

Sentiment Analysis:

AI-powered sentiment analysis can gauge market sentiment by analyzing social media posts, news articles, and other online content. Understanding market sentiment is crucial as it can impact asset prices and market movements. AI's ability to interpret sentiment aids investors in gauging market sentiment and adjusting their strategies accordingly.

Forecasting and Predictive Modeling:

AI models can be trained to forecast asset prices, market trends, and economic indicators. These predictive models help investors anticipate potential market movements and make more timely investment decisions.

Risk Management:

AI can assess portfolio risk and identify potential risks based on historical data and correlations between different assets. This enables investors to optimize their portfolios and implement risk management strategies effectively.

Automated Trading:

AI-driven automated trading systems execute trades based on predefined rules and algorithms. These systems can process real-time market data, identify trading opportunities, and execute trades at high speeds, improving trade execution efficiency.

Portfolio Optimization:

AI can optimize portfolios based on various factors, including risk tolerance, return objectives, and investment horizon. It can suggest diversified asset allocations to achieve better risk-adjusted returns.

Market Monitoring and Real-Time Updates:

AI-powered tools continuously monitor financial markets, providing real-time updates on market movements, news, and events. This ensures that investors have access to the latest information to make informed decisions.

Backtesting Strategies:

AI enables investors to backtest their investment strategies using historical market data. By evaluating the performance of strategies over time, investors can refine their approaches and identify potential weaknesses.

Identifying Investment Opportunities:

AI can scan a vast universe of investment opportunities, screening stocks, bonds, and other assets based on predefined criteria. This saves time and resources for investors, allowing them to focus on the most promising opportunities.

Personalized Investment Advice:

AI-driven robo-advisors provide personalized investment advice to individual investors based on their financial goals, risk tolerance, and investment preferences. This democratizes access to professional investment advice and management.

While AI brings significant advantages to investment decisions, it is crucial to acknowledge its limitations. AI models are built on historical data and assumptions, and unexpected events or black swan events may lead to unforeseen outcomes. Moreover, human expertise, judgment, and intuition remain invaluable in understanding the broader economic context and qualitative factors that AI may not fully capture.

AI's role in investment decisions is rapidly evolving, and its potential to enhance decision-making processes and optimize investment strategies is immense. By combining AI-driven insights with human expertise, investors can create a powerful synergy that leads to better-informed decisions, improved risk management, and enhanced portfolio performance. As AI technology continues to advance, the integration of AI in investment decisions will become even more sophisticated, contributing to a more efficient and robust global financial ecosystem.

Using ChatGPT for Stock Analysis and Portfolio Management

In the ever-evolving world of finance and investing, staying ahead of market trends and making informed decisions are crucial for successful stock analysis and portfolio management. The advent of artificial intelligence, particularly ChatGPT, has revolutionized the way investors approach stock analysis and portfolio optimization. ChatGPT, powered by natural language processing and machine learning, empowers investors with data-driven insights, real-time updates, and personalized portfolio recommendations. In this chapter, we will explore how ChatGPT can be utilized for stock analysis and portfolio management, helping investors make smarter and more strategic investment choices.

Real-Time Stock Analysis

ChatGPT's ability to process vast amounts of financial data, news, and market trends enables real-time stock analysis. By interpreting real-time market data and events, ChatGPT can offer immediate insights into stock movements, news-driven volatility, and potential opportunities or risks.

Sentiment Analysis

Sentiment analysis is a powerful tool in stock analysis, as market sentiment often influences stock prices. ChatGPT can analyze social media posts, news articles, and analyst reports to gauge market sentiment. Understanding sentiment can aid investors in making decisions based on market sentiment and potential shifts in stock prices.

Fundamental Analysis

ChatGPT can perform fundamental analysis by analyzing a company's financial statements, earnings reports, and key performance indicators. This helps investors assess a company's financial health, growth prospects, and intrinsic value, aiding in identifying undervalued or overvalued stocks.

Technical Analysis

Technical analysis involves studying historical price charts and patterns to predict future stock price movements. ChatGPT can assist in technical analysis by identifying trends, chart patterns, and support/resistance levels, providing investors with valuable insights for their trading decisions.

Risk Assessment

Effective risk management is essential for successful portfolio management. ChatGPT can assess portfolio risk by analyzing asset correlations, volatility, and market conditions. Investors can adjust their portfolio allocation based on ChatGPT's insights to achieve better risk-adjusted returns.

Portfolio Diversification

Diversification is a key tenet of portfolio management. ChatGPT can recommend diversified asset allocations based on investors' risk tolerance and investment goals. This helps mitigate concentration risk and enhances the overall stability of the portfolio.

Backtesting Strategies

Investors can use ChatGPT to backtest their investment strategies using historical market data. By evaluating the performance of strategies over time, investors can refine their approaches and identify potential weaknesses.

Portfolio Rebalancing

ChatGPT can assist in portfolio rebalancing by recommending adjustments based on changes in asset prices and market conditions. Regular portfolio rebalancing helps maintain the desired asset allocation and aligns the portfolio with the investor's long-term goals.

Personalized Portfolio Recommendations

ChatGPT can offer personalized portfolio recommendations based on investors' financial goals, risk tolerance, and time horizon. This provides individual investors with tailor-made investment strategies, similar to the advice offered by professional financial advisors.

Financial News Updates

Keeping abreast of financial news and developments is crucial for investors. ChatGPT can provide real-time updates on breaking news, earnings reports, economic indicators, and geopolitical events that may impact stock prices and the overall market.

Integrating ChatGPT into stock analysis and portfolio management offers a powerful advantage to investors, enabling them to make more informed and data-driven investment decisions. By leveraging ChatGPT's real-time analysis, sentiment analysis, fundamental and technical analysis, investors can gain valuable insights into the stock market and identify potential opportunities and risks.

ChatGPT's role in risk assessment, portfolio diversification, and portfolio rebalancing contributes to effective risk management and optimized portfolio performance. Its ability to perform personalized portfolio recommendations brings professional-level advice to individual investors, enhancing their investment experience.

However, it is crucial to recognize that AI tools, including ChatGPT, are not infallible. Unexpected market events and black swan events can lead to unforeseen outcomes, and human expertise remains invaluable in understanding qualitative factors that AI may not fully capture.

Investors must use ChatGPT as a powerful complement to their own research and expertise, rather than a replacement for human judgment. Moreover, data privacy and security are critical considerations when using AI-powered tools for stock analysis and portfolio management.

As AI technology continues to advance, the potential of ChatGPT in stock analysis and portfolio management will only expand, leading to more sophisticated and efficient investment strategies. By embracing ChatGPT's capabilities, investors can enhance their decision-making processes, optimize their portfolios, and navigate the complexities of the stock market with greater confidence and efficiency.

The integration of ChatGPT in stock analysis and portfolio management fosters financial inclusion by democratizing access to advanced investment tools. Previously, sophisticated analysis and portfolio management were predominantly available to institutional investors and high-net-worth individuals. However, ChatGPT's user-friendly interface and accessibility level the playing field, making data-driven insights and portfolio recommendations accessible to individual investors and retail traders.

ChatGPT serves as a valuable educational resource for novice investors, providing explanations of financial concepts and analysis in plain language. This empowers individuals to gain a deeper understanding of the stock market, investment strategies, and risk management principles. As investors interact with ChatGPT and receive personalized insights, they can gradually build their investment acumen and confidence, fostering a sense of empowerment in managing their financial future.

ChatGPT's analytical capabilities facilitate informed decision-making in investment strategies, such as value investing, growth investing, and dividend investing. Investors can combine their own investment philosophies with data-driven insights from ChatGPT to create well-rounded and robust strategies that align with their financial goals.

For institutional investors, ChatGPT acts as an augmentative tool for financial analysis and portfolio management. The integration of AI-powered insights with human expertise allows institutions to validate investment hypotheses, assess market sentiment, and identify alpha-generating opportunities more efficiently.

As with any AI-powered tool, it is crucial to exercise caution and not solely rely on ChatGPT's recommendations. The stock market is inherently unpredictable, and no AI model can predict future events with certainty. Investors must always approach investment decisions with a long-term perspective, diversification, and risk management strategies to navigate market fluctuations and uncertainties.

Moreover, ensuring data privacy and security is paramount when utilizing AI-powered tools for financial analysis. Investors must be vigilant in protecting sensitive financial information and ensure that the AI platform adheres to robust data protection measures.

ChatGPT's integration into stock analysis and portfolio management has reshaped the way investors approach financial decision-making. Its real-time analysis, sentiment analysis, fundamental and technical analysis, and personalized portfolio recommendations offer valuable insights to investors of all levels. By combining AI-driven insights with human expertise, investors can make well-informed investment decisions, optimize their portfolios, and manage risk more effectively.

ChatGPT contributes to financial inclusion by providing sophisticated investment tools and education to individual investors, leveling the playing field in the world of finance. However, investors must exercise prudent judgment and recognize that human expertise remains indispensable in understanding qualitative factors and navigating unexpected market events.

As AI technology continues to advance, the potential for ChatGPT and other AI-powered tools in stock analysis and portfolio management will continue to grow. By embracing AI responsibly, investors can harness the full potential of technology to improve their investment outcomes and achieve their financial goals. Whether used by individual investors or institutional professionals, ChatGPT represents a transformative force that drives the financial industry towards a more data-driven, accessible, and inclusive future.

Automating cryptocurrency trading with ChatGPT algorithms

Automating cryptocurrency trading with ChatGPT algorithms has emerged as a popular approach among traders seeking to capitalize on the dynamic nature of the cryptocurrency markets. By combining the language generation capabilities of ChatGPT with advanced machine learning algorithms, traders can create sophisticated trading strategies that adapt to real-time market conditions. Here's a comprehensive overview of how ChatGPT algorithms can be used to automate cryptocurrency trading:

Data Analysis and Market Insights:

ChatGPT's natural language processing capabilities enable it to analyze vast amounts of financial news, social media chatter, and market data related to cryptocurrencies. By processing and interpreting this data, ChatGPT algorithms can extract valuable market insights and sentiment analysis to gauge market sentiment.

Algorithmic Trading Strategies:

Traders can develop and implement algorithmic trading strategies based on ChatGPT-generated insights. These strategies can range from simple rules-based approaches to more complex machine learning models that continually learn and adapt to market changes.

Real-Time Trading Signals:

ChatGPT algorithms can generate real-time trading signals based on technical indicators, sentiment analysis, and market trends. These signals can prompt the automated execution of buy or sell orders, allowing traders to respond swiftly to market opportunities.

Risk Management:

Effective risk management is crucial in cryptocurrency trading due to the high volatility of the markets. ChatGPT algorithms can incorporate risk management rules, such as stop-loss orders and position sizing, to protect capital and minimize potential losses.

Portfolio Diversification:

ChatGPT algorithms can recommend diversified cryptocurrency portfolios based on risk tolerance and investment objectives. By considering correlations between different cryptocurrencies, the algorithms can optimize portfolio allocations to achieve better risk-adjusted returns.

Backtesting and Optimization:

Before deploying ChatGPT algorithms in live trading, traders can backtest their strategies using historical cryptocurrency market data. Backtesting allows traders to assess the performance of their algorithms in different market conditions and optimize their strategies for better results.

Emotion-Free Trading:

Automated trading with ChatGPT algorithms eliminates emotional biases that can influence human decision-making. Emotion-free trading helps maintain discipline and adherence to predefined trading rules.

Continual Learning:

Machine learning algorithms integrated with ChatGPT can continuously learn from new market data and adjust their trading strategies accordingly. This adaptability allows the algorithms to stay relevant and effective in ever-changing market conditions.

Trade Execution and Order Management:

ChatGPT algorithms can interface with cryptocurrency exchanges to execute trades and manage orders automatically. This streamlines the trading process and ensures that trading decisions are promptly executed.

Constant Monitoring:

Automated trading systems require continuous monitoring to ensure they are functioning correctly. Traders need to regularly check their algorithms, verify their performance, and make adjustments if necessary.

Automating cryptocurrency trading with ChatGPT algorithms has become a game-changer for traders seeking to capitalize on the fast-paced and highly volatile nature of the cryptocurrency markets. By leveraging ChatGPT's language generation capabilities and combining them with advanced machine learning algorithms, traders can gain valuable insights, execute real-time trading strategies, and optimize their portfolios for better risk-adjusted returns.

However, it is essential to recognize that cryptocurrency markets are inherently risky and subject to sudden price fluctuations. Traders must exercise caution and carefully consider the risks associated with automated trading. Implementing proper risk management strategies and conducting thorough testing and optimization of ChatGPT algorithms are crucial steps in building a successful automated cryptocurrency trading system.

Overall, the integration of ChatGPT algorithms in cryptocurrency trading represents a significant step forward in the evolution of automated trading systems, providing traders with a powerful tool to navigate the complexities of the cryptocurrency markets and potentially achieve more consistent and profitable outcomes.

The automation of cryptocurrency trading with ChatGPT algorithms offers several advantages to traders and investors:

Speed and Efficiency: Automated trading with ChatGPT algorithms allows for swift and precise execution of trades, responding to market opportunities in real-time. The algorithms can process vast amounts of data and execute orders at speeds impossible for human traders.

Elimination of Emotional Bias: Emotional biases, such as fear and greed, can lead to impulsive and irrational trading decisions. By automating trading with ChatGPT algorithms, emotions are removed from the equation, leading to more disciplined and objective trading strategies.

24/7 Market Monitoring: Cryptocurrency markets operate 24/7, which can be challenging for human traders to monitor continuously. ChatGPT algorithms can constantly analyze market data, even during non-trading hours, ensuring that no potential opportunities or risks are missed.

Improved Trade Execution: Automated trading eliminates the possibility of execution delays or manual errors, ensuring that trades are executed precisely according to the predefined rules.

Enhanced Risk Management: ChatGPT algorithms can incorporate risk management parameters, such as stop-loss and take-profit orders, to protect against significant losses and secure profits.

Multi-Market Analysis: Cryptocurrency traders often monitor multiple markets simultaneously. ChatGPT algorithms can analyze and trade across various cryptocurrencies and exchanges, diversifying trading opportunities and optimizing the potential for profit.

Data-Driven Decision-Making: ChatGPT algorithms rely on data-driven insights and analysis, helping traders make more informed decisions based on market trends and sentiment.

However, it is essential to be mindful of the potential challenges and risks associated with automated cryptocurrency trading:

Overfitting: While backtesting is crucial for evaluating algorithm performance, it can lead to overfitting - a situation where an algorithm performs well in historical data but poorly in real-time conditions. Traders must ensure their algorithms are robust and can adapt to changing market conditions.

Technology and Connectivity Risks: Automated trading systems are reliant on stable internet connections and reliable technology. Technical failures or connectivity issues can disrupt trading operations and lead to potential losses.

Market Liquidity: In less liquid cryptocurrency markets, automated trading can lead to slippage - a situation where the executed price differs significantly from the desired price due to market fluctuations.

Regulatory Compliance: Traders must be aware of the regulatory environment surrounding cryptocurrency trading, as automated trading systems need to adhere to relevant laws and guidelines.

Lack of Human Judgment: While automation can remove emotional biases, it also means that critical human judgment and intuition are absent. There may be situations where a human trader's qualitative analysis could provide valuable insights that automated systems cannot replicate.

Automating cryptocurrency trading with ChatGPT algorithms represents a powerful and innovative approach to navigating the dynamic and highly volatile cryptocurrency markets. By leveraging the capabilities of ChatGPT's language generation and advanced machine learning algorithms, traders can gain valuable insights, optimize trading strategies, and improve risk management.

Automated trading offers speed, efficiency, and emotion-free decision-making, but it is not without challenges and risks. Traders must approach automated trading with careful consideration, conducting rigorous testing, and implementing robust risk management strategies.

Ultimately, the successful integration of ChatGPT algorithms in cryptocurrency trading requires a balanced approach that combines the benefits of automation with the valuable judgment and expertise of human traders. As technology continues to advance, the potential of ChatGPT algorithms in automated cryptocurrency trading will expand, presenting traders with new opportunities to enhance their trading strategies and achieve better outcomes in the dynamic world of cryptocurrencies.

7. ChatGPT and the Gig Economy

The gig economy, characterized by temporary and flexible work arrangements, has experienced significant growth in recent years. Technology plays a pivotal role in shaping the gig economy, and the integration of artificial intelligence, particularly ChatGPT, has further transformed the landscape. In this chapter, we will explore how ChatGPT is reshaping the gig economy, empowering gig workers, and providing innovative solutions to gig-based businesses.

Virtual Gig Assistants

ChatGPT serves as a virtual gig assistant, enabling gig workers to streamline their tasks, manage schedules, and communicate with clients efficiently. With natural language processing capabilities, ChatGPT can handle client inquiries, schedule appointments, and even assist with project coordination, allowing gig workers to focus on core tasks.

Resume Writing and Personal Branding

For freelancers and independent contractors, personal branding is essential to attract clients and secure gigs. ChatGPT can aid gig workers in crafting compelling resumes and building strong online profiles, showcasing their skills and expertise effectively.

Skill Development and Training

The gig economy demands a diverse set of skills, and gig workers need to continuously upgrade their capabilities to stay competitive. ChatGPT can act as a personalized learning resource, providing gig workers with educational content, skill development resources, and career guidance.

Matching Gig Workers with Jobs

ChatGPT algorithms can match gig workers with relevant job opportunities based on their skills and preferences. This efficient matchmaking process benefits both gig workers, who find suitable gigs, and businesses seeking talented individuals for their projects.

Freelance Writing and Content Creation

ChatGPT's language generation capabilities have significant implications for the gig economy's content creation sector. Freelance writers and content creators can use ChatGPT to generate drafts, brainstorm ideas, and optimize content for SEO, streamlining their writing process.

AI-Enhanced Gig Platforms

Gig-based platforms can integrate ChatGPT to enhance user experiences. By offering virtual assistance to gig workers and clients, these platforms can improve communication, automate routine tasks, and facilitate a more efficient gig marketplace.

Customer Support and Chatbots

Gig-based businesses can employ ChatGPT-driven chatbots to provide customer support to their users. These chatbots can handle customer inquiries, assist with troubleshooting, and offer quick resolutions, enhancing user satisfaction and reducing the workload of gig workers.

Personal Finance Management

For gig workers managing fluctuating income streams, personal finance management can be challenging. ChatGPT can provide financial insights, budgeting tips, and investment advice, helping gig workers achieve greater financial stability.

Gig Worker Well-Being

The gig economy can be demanding, leading to stress and burnout for gig workers. ChatGPT can offer mental health resources, stress management techniques, and work-life balance suggestions to support gig worker well-being.

Gig Economy Policy and Regulation

AI-powered tools like ChatGPT can play a role in shaping gig economy policies and regulations. By analyzing gig worker data and feedback, policymakers can gain valuable insights to inform decisions that protect gig worker rights and promote fair labor practices.

ChatGPT's integration into the gig economy has ushered in a new era of opportunities and efficiencies for gig workers and businesses alike. As a virtual gig assistant, skill development resource, and content creation tool, ChatGPT empowers gig workers to thrive in the gig economy's dynamic landscape.

For gig-based businesses, ChatGPT-driven solutions offer streamlined operations, enhanced user experiences, and improved customer support. By embracing ChatGPT, the gig economy is poised to become more efficient, inclusive, and supportive of gig workers' needs and aspirations.

However, it is essential to recognize the potential challenges of integrating AI in the gig economy. Concerns over data privacy, algorithmic bias, and gig worker autonomy must be addressed to ensure a fair and ethical application of ChatGPT in the gig economy.

As technology continues to evolve, the potential of ChatGPT and AI in the gig economy will expand, presenting new possibilities for gig workers and businesses to thrive in the ever-evolving world of flexible work arrangements. By embracing AI responsibly and maintaining a human-centric approach, the gig economy can harness the full potential of ChatGPT to create a more sustainable, innovative, and empowering gig ecosystem.

Exploring freelance opportunities with ChatGPT skills

Freelancers with ChatGPT skills have a wide range of exciting opportunities in various industries. As the demand for AI-driven solutions and natural language processing continues to grow, these skills become increasingly valuable. Here are some freelance opportunities for individuals with ChatGPT skills:

Content Creation and Writing:

Freelance writers and content creators can leverage ChatGPT's language generation capabilities to streamline their writing process. They can use ChatGPT to brainstorm ideas, generate drafts, and optimize content for SEO, allowing them to deliver high-quality content efficiently.

Social Media Management:

ChatGPT can assist freelance social media managers in crafting engaging posts and content for social media platforms. By using ChatGPT to generate creative and captivating content, social media managers can enhance their clients' online presence and audience engagement.

Virtual Assistant Services:

As a virtual gig assistant, freelancers with ChatGPT skills can offer virtual assistant services to clients. They can manage schedules, handle client inquiries, and coordinate tasks, providing efficient and effective support to businesses and entrepreneurs.

Resume Writing and Personal Branding:

Freelancers can use ChatGPT to help clients craft compelling resumes and build strong online profiles. By leveraging ChatGPT's language generation capabilities, freelancers can create personalized and impactful resumes that stand out to potential employers.

Customer Support and Chatbots:

Freelancers can develop AI-driven chatbots for businesses to enhance their customer support services. Chatbots can handle customer inquiries, troubleshoot issues, and provide quick resolutions, reducing the workload for businesses and improving customer satisfaction.

E-commerce Product Descriptions:

E-commerce businesses often require engaging product descriptions to attract customers. Freelancers can use ChatGPT to generate product descriptions that are informative, persuasive, and tailored to the target audience.

Language Translation Services:

ChatGPT's language capabilities extend to translation services. Freelancers with ChatGPT skills can offer language translation services for businesses and individuals looking to communicate with a global audience.

Market Research and Insights:

Freelancers can assist businesses with market research and insights using ChatGPT's data analysis and natural language processing capabilities. By analyzing market trends and consumer sentiments, freelancers can provide valuable insights for strategic decision-making.

Personal Finance and Investment Advice:

Individuals with ChatGPT skills can offer personalized financial advice and investment recommendations to clients. ChatGPT's ability to analyze financial data and offer insights can aid clients in making informed decisions about their finances.

Customized Educational Content:

Freelancers can create customized educational content using ChatGPT for various industries and educational purposes. This content can include tutorials, guides, and learning resources tailored to the specific needs of clients and learners.

Freelancers with ChatGPT skills are well-positioned to capitalize on the growing demand for AI-driven solutions and language generation capabilities across various industries. Whether it's content creation, virtual assistant services, customer support, or market research, ChatGPT skills offer valuable opportunities to thrive in the freelance market.

As technology continues to evolve, the potential for ChatGPT skills in the freelance market will expand even further. By staying updated with the latest advancements in AI and continuously honing their ChatGPT skills, freelancers can stay at the forefront of the gig economy and offer innovative solutions to meet the evolving needs of clients and businesses.

As freelancers with ChatGPT skills explore opportunities in various industries, it's essential to highlight the benefits they bring to clients and businesses:

Cost-Effectiveness: ChatGPT skills enable freelancers to automate certain tasks and processes, reducing manual efforts and saving time for clients. This cost-effectiveness appeals to businesses looking to optimize their operations without the need for extensive resources.

Increased Efficiency: With ChatGPT's language generation capabilities, freelancers can produce content and deliver services more efficiently. The ability to generate drafts, brainstorm ideas, and handle routine tasks allows freelancers to focus on providing higher-value services to their clients.

Personalization: Freelancers can leverage ChatGPT to provide personalized and tailored solutions to their clients. Whether it's creating customized content or offering personalized advice, ChatGPT skills enable freelancers to meet the unique needs of individual clients.

Scalability: ChatGPT allows freelancers to handle multiple clients and projects simultaneously, facilitating scalability in their freelance business. The ability to manage schedules, communication, and content creation efficiently means freelancers can take on more projects without compromising quality.

Innovation: Offering AI-driven solutions through ChatGPT skills demonstrates a freelancer's commitment to staying at the cutting edge of technology. Clients and businesses are increasingly seeking innovative approaches, and freelancers with ChatGPT skills can provide unique and forward-thinking solutions.

Streamlined Communication: ChatGPT can act as a virtual assistant, facilitating communication between freelancers and their clients. Quick response times and efficient handling of client inquiries contribute to a seamless client experience.

Niche Specialization: Freelancers can use ChatGPT skills to specialize in niche areas, where the demand for AI-driven solutions is particularly high. This specialization can set them apart from competitors and attract clients seeking specialized expertise.

Client Retention: By providing valuable and data-driven insights through ChatGPT, freelancers can enhance client satisfaction and retention. Satisfied clients are more likely to return for additional services and refer freelancers to others.

Access to New Markets: ChatGPT skills open doors to industries and sectors where AI-driven solutions are increasingly in demand. Freelancers can tap into new markets and diversify their client base, expanding their reach and opportunities.

Continuous Learning and Growth: Embracing ChatGPT skills allows freelancers to engage in continuous learning and skill development. As AI technology advances, staying up-to-date with ChatGPT capabilities ensures freelancers remain relevant and competitive in the market.

Freelancers with ChatGPT skills have a plethora of opportunities to explore in the gig economy. From content creation and virtual assistant services to customer support and market research, ChatGPT skills offer innovative and efficient solutions to businesses and clients across various industries.

As freelancers continue to harness the power of AI and ChatGPT, they can elevate their freelance careers, attract a broader client base, and establish themselves as experts in their fields. The potential for ChatGPT skills in the freelance market is limitless, presenting freelancers with a world of possibilities to thrive in the dynamic and ever-evolving gig economy. By embracing technology responsibly and continuously honing their ChatGPT skills, freelancers can unlock the full potential of AI to deliver exceptional value and drive their freelance businesses to new heights.

Offering AI-powered services on online platforms

Offering AI-powered services on online platforms can be a lucrative and innovative venture for freelancers and businesses alike. As AI technology continues to advance, the demand for AI-driven solutions is increasing across various industries. Here's a guide on how to offer AI-powered services on online platforms:

Identify Your AI Expertise: Determine your specific AI expertise and the services you can offer. This could include natural language processing, machine learning, computer vision, chatbot development, data analysis, or any other AI-related field. Specializing in a niche area will help you stand out and attract clients seeking specialized solutions.

Create a Portfolio: Showcase your AI projects and accomplishments in a portfolio. Include case studies, samples of your work, and testimonials from satisfied clients. A well-structured portfolio will demonstrate your skills and expertise to potential clients on online platforms.

Choose the Right Online Platform: There are numerous online platforms where you can offer your AI-powered services. Some popular options include freelance marketplaces like Upwork, Fiverr, and Freelancer, as well as AI-specific platforms like OpenAI's marketplace or specialized industry-specific platforms.

Craft a Compelling Profile: Create a compelling profile that highlights your AI skills, experience, and achievements. Use keywords related to AI and your niche specialization to make it easier for potential clients to find you when searching for AI services.

Set Competitive Pricing: Determine competitive pricing for your AI services based on your expertise, the complexity of the projects, and market rates. Offering transparent and reasonable pricing will attract clients and build trust in your services.

Offer Customized Solutions: Tailor your AI services to the specific needs of each client. Listen to their requirements and provide personalized solutions that address their unique challenges. Customization will set you apart from generic AI service providers.

Provide Clear Deliverables: Clearly outline the deliverables and milestones in your service packages. Be transparent about the expected outcomes and timelines to manage client expectations effectively.

Communicate Value Proposition: Clearly communicate the value of your AI-powered services to potential clients. Explain how AI can solve their problems, optimize processes, and improve efficiency in their businesses.

Offer Support and Training: Some clients may be new to AI technology and require guidance on using your AI solutions effectively. Offer post-service support, training, and documentation to help clients make the most out of your AI services.

Build Relationships and Referrals: Deliver exceptional AI solutions and build strong relationships with your clients. Satisfied clients are more likely to refer you to others, leading to organic growth for your AI-powered service business.

Offering AI-powered services on online platforms is an excellent way to capitalize on the growing demand for AI-driven solutions. By showcasing your expertise, creating a compelling profile, and customizing your services, you can attract clients seeking AI solutions for their businesses. Providing value, support, and building strong client relationships will lead to a successful and thriving AI-powered service business in the online marketplace. As AI technology continues to evolve, staying up-to-date with the latest advancements will keep you at the forefront of the industry and position you as a go-to expert for AI solutions.

Here are additional steps to solidify your position and thrive in the online marketplace:

Demonstrate Real-World Applications: Showcase real-world applications of your AI solutions through case studies or success stories. Highlight how your services have positively impacted clients' businesses, such as improving efficiency, increasing revenue, or enhancing customer experience.

Stay Updated with AI Trends: AI technology is ever-evolving, with new advancements and breakthroughs occurring regularly. Stay updated with the latest AI trends, research, and tools to ensure your services are at the forefront of innovation.

Collaborate and Network: Collaborate with other AI experts and professionals to expand your knowledge base and foster networking opportunities. Engaging with AI communities, forums, and industry events can lead to valuable partnerships and project collaborations.

Offer Trial Periods: Provide potential clients with trial periods or demo versions of your AI solutions. Allowing them to experience the benefits firsthand can encourage them to commit to your services.

Collect and Showcase Testimonials: Positive feedback from satisfied clients can significantly impact your credibility. Request testimonials from clients who have benefited from your AI services, and prominently display them on your profile and

Managing workload and scaling your gig business

Managing workload and scaling your gig business are crucial aspects of ensuring sustained success and growth as a freelancer. As the demand for your services increases, efficiently managing your workload and expanding your operations become essential. Here are some strategies to help you effectively handle your workload and scale your gig business:

Time Management: Implement effective time management techniques to prioritize tasks, set deadlines, and allocate sufficient time for each project. Use time management tools and techniques to ensure you meet client expectations and deliver high-quality work on time.

Set Realistic Goals: Define clear and achievable business goals to guide your efforts. Break down larger objectives into smaller, manageable tasks, and celebrate milestones as you achieve them. Setting realistic goals will prevent overwhelm and help you stay focused on your growth trajectory.

Outsource or Collaborate: As your gig business scales, consider outsourcing or collaborating with other freelancers or professionals. Delegating certain tasks can free up time for you to focus on core areas of your business while still meeting client demands.

Automate Routine Tasks: Use automation tools to streamline repetitive tasks, such as invoicing, project tracking, or client communication. Automation saves time and allows you to focus on value-added activities.

Build a Reliable Support System: Establish a network of reliable contacts, such as virtual assistants, project managers, or contractors, who can support you during periods of high workload. Having a support system ensures that you can handle multiple projects efficiently.

Expand Your Skill Set: Invest in continuous learning and expand your skill set to diversify the services you offer. This enables you to cater to a broader client base and tackle more complex projects.

Standardize Processes: Develop standardized processes for project onboarding, execution, and delivery. Streamlining your workflows enhances efficiency and consistency, making it easier to manage multiple projects simultaneously.

Implement Scalable Pricing: Develop a pricing structure that accounts for scalability. As your gig business grows, ensure that your pricing aligns with the value you offer while accommodating the increased demand for your services.

Seek Feedback: Regularly seek feedback from clients to gauge their satisfaction with your services. Constructive feedback allows you to make improvements and build stronger client relationships.

Branding and Marketing: Invest in branding and marketing efforts to increase your visibility and attract new clients. Utilize social media, content marketing, and networking to showcase your expertise and expand your client base.

Client Relationship Management: Nurture strong relationships with existing clients by offering exceptional service and personalized attention. Satisfied clients are more likely to become repeat customers and refer others to your services.

Plan for Growth: Develop a growth strategy and plan ahead for scaling your gig business. Anticipate future challenges and opportunities, and create a roadmap to achieve your long-term business objectives.

Managing workload and scaling your gig business require careful planning, efficient time management, and a commitment to continuous improvement. By implementing these strategies and staying responsive to market demands, you can effectively handle increased workload, deliver quality services, and expand your gig business successfully. Scaling your business sustainably will position you for long-term success and increased recognition as a trusted expert in your field.

8. ChatGPT and Social Media Influence

Social media has become an integral part of modern life, shaping how people connect, share information, and engage with content. As the influence of social media continues to grow, so does the role of AI in optimizing content creation, engagement strategies, and audience interactions. In this chapter, we will explore the intersection of ChatGPT and social media influence, examining how AI-driven insights and strategies can enhance social media presence and impact.

Content Creation and Optimization:

ChatGPT's language generation capabilities offer invaluable support for social media content creators. From generating catchy headlines to crafting engaging captions and posts, ChatGPT can help influencers maintain a consistent flow of compelling content. Moreover, AI-driven data analysis can identify trending topics and optimize content to resonate with target audiences.

Social Media Engagement:

Understanding audience behavior is critical for influencers looking to boost engagement on social media platforms. ChatGPT's sentiment analysis and audience insights can help influencers tailor their content to meet audience preferences and effectively interact with followers. AI-driven chatbots also enhance responsiveness, ensuring prompt replies to inquiries and comments.

Influencer Marketing Strategies:

AI-powered analytics enable influencers to make informed decisions about partnerships and collaborations. By analyzing the performance of sponsored content and influencer marketing campaigns, influencers can identify which collaborations generate the most significant impact and ROI.

Personalized Audience Interaction:

ChatGPT can personalize audience interactions by recommending content, responding to comments, and offering tailored recommendations. This personalized approach strengthens the bond between influencers and their followers, increasing brand loyalty and audience engagement.

Social Listening and Trend Analysis:

AI-powered tools can conduct social listening and trend analysis, helping influencers stay attuned to audience sentiments and emerging topics. This valuable insight aids in adapting content strategies and staying relevant in dynamic social media landscapes.

Crisis Management:

In times of crisis or controversy, ChatGPT-driven sentiment analysis can help influencers gauge public opinion and respond accordingly. By understanding audience sentiment, influencers can address concerns and manage potential reputational risks more effectively.

Influencer Fraud Detection:

AI algorithms can help detect and prevent influencer fraud, ensuring genuine and authentic influencer partnerships. By analyzing engagement metrics and detecting suspicious patterns, brands can make more informed decisions when selecting influencers.

Social Media Advertising:

ChatGPT can optimize social media advertising by generating persuasive ad copy and identifying target audience segments. AI-driven insights enable influencers and businesses to enhance the effectiveness of their ad campaigns.

Social Media Performance Analytics:

AI-powered analytics tools can provide comprehensive performance reports, enabling influencers to track key metrics and measure the impact of their social media efforts. This data-driven approach informs future content strategies and engagement tactics.

Enhancing Social Media Creativity:

AI, including ChatGPT, can act as a creative assistant, inspiring influencers with innovative ideas and unique content concepts. By collaborating with AI, influencers can explore new creative directions and experiment with diverse content formats.

ChatGPT's integration into social media influence has revolutionized the way influencers connect with their audiences and create content. AI-driven insights, analytics, and personalized interactions have become indispensable tools for optimizing social media presence and impact. As the influence of social media continues to shape online interactions, influencers and businesses alike must embrace AI-powered tools to stay relevant, authentic, and engaging in the fast-paced world of social media. Through responsible and strategic utilization of ChatGPT and AI, social media influencers can elevate their influence, expand their reach, and build lasting connections with their audiences.

Enhancing social media presence with AI-generated content

Enhancing social media presence with AI-generated content has become a powerful strategy for influencers, businesses, and brands seeking to maintain a consistent and engaging online presence. AI, particularly ChatGPT, offers various ways to optimize content creation, drive audience engagement, and amplify social media impact. Here are the key ways AI-generated content can enhance social media presence:

Streamlined Content Creation: ChatGPT's language generation capabilities allow influencers and marketers to generate content quickly and efficiently. From writing blog posts to creating social media captions, AI-generated content streamlines the content creation process, ensuring a steady flow of fresh and engaging material.

Personalized Audience Interaction: AI-powered chatbots can personalize audience interactions by responding to comments, messages, and inquiries. This level of responsiveness enhances the user experience and fosters stronger connections with followers, leading to increased brand loyalty.

Trend Analysis and Optimization: AI can analyze social media trends and recommend content topics that are likely to resonate with the target audience. By tapping into trending topics, influencers can stay relevant and increase the visibility of their content.

Multilingual Content: ChatGPT can create content in multiple languages, allowing influencers and brands to expand their reach to a global audience. This multilingual approach enables them to connect with diverse communities and international markets.

Content Repurposing: AI-generated content can be repurposed for various social media platforms and formats. For instance, a blog post can be transformed into social media graphics or short video clips, maximizing the content's reach and impact.

A/B Testing and Optimization: AI can facilitate A/B testing of different content variations, helping influencers identify which type of content performs best with their audience. This data-driven approach empowers them to optimize content strategies for maximum engagement.

Personal Branding and Voice: AI-generated content can capture an influencer's unique voice and style, maintaining consistency across social media platforms. This ensures that the influencer's personal brand is effectively conveyed to followers.

Social Media Advertising: AI-generated content can be leveraged in social media advertising campaigns to create persuasive ad copy and optimize ad performance. AI insights enable advertisers to target specific audience segments effectively.

Real-time Content Updates: AI can monitor real-time events and generate content that aligns with current news or trends. This agility allows influencers to seize timely opportunities and create content that resonates with ongoing conversations.

Diverse Content Formats: ChatGPT can assist influencers in creating various content formats, such as blog posts, infographics, videos, and podcasts. Diversifying content formats keeps the audience engaged and attracts different types of viewers.

AI-generated content has transformed the social media landscape, empowering influencers, businesses, and brands to enhance their online presence and impact. By leveraging ChatGPT's language generation capabilities, social media stakeholders can streamline content creation, engage with their audience on a more personal level, and optimize their social media strategies based on data-driven insights.

However, it's essential to maintain a balance between AI-generated content and authentic human engagement. While AI can enhance efficiency and creativity, human input and genuine interactions remain crucial for building meaningful connections with followers. Responsible and strategic use of AI-generated content ensures that influencers and brands maintain an authentic and influential presence in the dynamic world of social media.

Attracting followers and engagement through ChatGPT insights

Attracting followers and increasing engagement are key goals for influencers and businesses on social media platforms. By leveraging ChatGPT insights, influencers can optimize their content strategies and create more compelling and relevant posts to captivate their audience. Here's how ChatGPT insights can help attract followers and boost engagement:

Understanding Audience Preferences: ChatGPT's data analysis capabilities can provide valuable insights into audience preferences, interests, and behaviors. By understanding what content resonates best with their followers, influencers can tailor their posts to cater to their audience's specific interests.

Trend Analysis and Timely Content: ChatGPT can identify trending topics and conversations on social media. By creating content that aligns with current trends and timely events, influencers can increase their visibility and attract new followers who are interested in the latest discussions.

Crafting Compelling Headlines: ChatGPT can assist in generating attention-grabbing headlines and captions for social media posts. An enticing headline piques the curiosity of users and encourages them to click through to read the full content, boosting engagement rates.

Improving Content Relevance: Through AI-generated insights, influencers can gain a deeper understanding of the topics and themes that resonate most with their audience. This helps them create content that is highly relevant and valuable to their followers, leading to increased engagement and loyalty.

Analyzing Optimal Posting Times: ChatGPT can analyze engagement patterns and suggest optimal posting times based on when the audience is most active. Posting at peak engagement times ensures that content reaches a broader audience and garners more interactions.

Responding to Audience Feedback: AI-driven sentiment analysis can help influencers gauge audience sentiment towards their content. By responding to positive feedback and addressing concerns promptly, influencers can foster a positive and engaged community.

Personalized Content Recommendations: ChatGPT can recommend personalized content based on user preferences and past interactions. Providing tailored content enhances user experience, making followers feel valued and more likely to engage with future posts.

Predicting User Intent: AI insights can predict user intent and what kind of content users are likely to engage with. By aligning content with user intent, influencers can create content that speaks directly to their audience's needs and interests.

Leveraging Influential Keywords: ChatGPT can identify influential keywords and hashtags that are trending or have high engagement rates. Incorporating these keywords in content increases the likelihood of discovery by new users and enhances content visibility.

Storytelling and Emotional Appeal: AI-generated insights can guide influencers on crafting compelling stories and emotional narratives. Storytelling evokes emotional responses from followers, leading to higher engagement and increased sharing of content.

Leveraging ChatGPT insights is a powerful strategy for attracting followers and boosting engagement on social media platforms. By understanding audience preferences, creating timely and relevant content, and utilizing influential keywords, influencers can optimize their content strategies to resonate with their target audience.

With AI-driven data analysis, influencers can make data-informed decisions and continuously improve their content to meet the evolving needs and interests of their followers. By delivering personalized, compelling, and emotionally resonant content, influencers can attract a loyal and engaged following, solidifying their position as influential figures on social media. The integration of ChatGPT insights into content creation and engagement strategies is a game-changer for influencers seeking to maximize their social media presence and impact.

Embracing Visual Storytelling: ChatGPT can provide insights into the types of visuals that resonate best with the audience. Influencers can use this information to create visually appealing content, such as images, infographics, and videos, to convey their brand message effectively.

Interactive Content: AI-driven insights can guide influencers in creating interactive content, such as polls, quizzes, and contests. Interactive elements encourage active participation from followers and increase engagement rates.

Influencer Collaborations: ChatGPT can analyze audience overlaps and recommend potential collaboration opportunities with other influencers. Collaborating with like-minded influencers exposes content to new audiences, leading to increased followers and engagement.

Monitoring Competitors: AI insights can be used to track and analyze competitor performance on social media. By understanding what works well for competitors and learning from their successes and mistakes, influencers can refine their own content strategies.

Aesthetic Consistency: ChatGPT insights can guide influencers in maintaining a consistent visual aesthetic and tone across their social media profiles. Consistency fosters brand recognition and trust among followers.

Gamification: ChatGPT can assist in developing gamified content that encourages users to participate in challenges, puzzles, or interactive stories. Gamification adds an element of fun and excitement, motivating followers to engage with the content more actively.

Emotional Analysis: AI can analyze the emotional impact of content on followers. Influencers can use this data to fine-tune their content to elicit specific emotions and forge deeper connections with their audience.

Story Sequencing: ChatGPT can suggest content sequencing to create compelling narratives that unfold over multiple posts. Sequential storytelling keeps followers engaged and eager to follow the progression of the story.

Evergreen Content Strategy: AI insights can identify evergreen content that continues to be relevant and valuable to the audience over time. Integrating evergreen content into the content strategy ensures a consistent stream of engaging posts.

Data-Driven Iteration: AI-generated insights provide valuable data for influencers to assess the performance of their content continuously. Using data-driven iteration, influencers can refine their strategies, identify what works best, and adapt to changing audience preferences.

Leveraging ChatGPT insights allows influencers to take their social media presence to new heights. By creating content that aligns with audience preferences, utilizing influential keywords, and implementing interactive and visually appealing elements, influencers can attract a growing and engaged following.

Data-driven decisions, continuous improvement, and audience-focused strategies are instrumental in sustaining long-term engagement and building a loyal community of followers. As influencers embrace AI-powered insights, they can optimize their content strategies, maintain relevance in the fast-paced world of social media, and solidify their position as influential figures who connect deeply with their audience.

Collaborating with brands for sponsored posts and promotions

Collaborating with brands for sponsored posts and promotions is a common and lucrative avenue for influencers to monetize their social media presence. Brands seek to leverage influencers' engaged and loyal following to reach their target audience authentically. As an influencer, here's how you can effectively collaborate with brands for sponsored posts and promotions:

Define Your Niche and Audience: Clearly define your niche and understand your audience demographics, interests, and preferences. Brands are more likely to collaborate with influencers whose content aligns with their target market.

Establish a Strong Brand Identity: Develop a consistent brand identity across your social media platforms. Showcase your unique voice, style, and aesthetic to build a recognizable personal brand that resonates with both followers and potential brand partners.

Demonstrate Engagement and Influence: Highlight your engagement rates, follower growth, and other relevant metrics to demonstrate your influence as an influencer. Brands are more inclined to collaborate with influencers who have an engaged and active audience.

Curate High-Quality Content: Showcase your content creation skills through high-quality posts and visuals. Brands seek influencers who can create appealing and compelling content that aligns with their brand values.

Reach Out to Brands: Proactively reach out to brands that align with your niche and values. Craft personalized pitches that outline the benefits of a collaboration and how your audience can positively impact their brand.

Showcase Previous Brand Collaborations: If you have previously worked with brands, showcase those collaborations and highlight the results and positive outcomes. Social proof of successful partnerships can attract more brands to collaborate with you.

Be Transparent and Authentic: Transparency is crucial in sponsored posts. Clearly disclose when a post is sponsored, and maintain authenticity in your collaborations. Followers appreciate genuine recommendations and honest reviews.

Align with Brand Objectives: Understand the brand's objectives and goals for the collaboration. Tailor your content to align with their campaign message and values to create a seamless partnership.

Negotiate Fair Compensation: Discuss compensation terms openly and negotiate fair rates for your sponsored posts and promotions. Consider factors such as deliverables, exclusivity, and usage rights when determining your fees.

Deliver on Commitments: Once you agree to collaborate, deliver the content as per the agreed-upon schedule and quality. Meeting or exceeding brand expectations enhances your reputation as a reliable and professional influencer.

Measure and Share Results: Provide brands with insights into the performance of your sponsored posts, including engagement metrics and any tangible impact on brand awareness or sales. This data reinforces your value as a brand partner.

Foster Long-Term Partnerships: If a collaboration is successful, nurture long-term partnerships with brands. Repeat collaborations with the same brands can lead to more significant opportunities and stable income streams.

Collaborating with brands for sponsored posts and promotions is an excellent way for influencers to monetize their social media influence and create mutually beneficial partnerships. By showcasing their unique brand identity, engagement, and content creation skills, influencers can attract brands that align with their niche and audience. Transparent and authentic collaborations, combined with a focus on delivering value, can lead to long-term and fruitful partnerships with brands in the dynamic world of influencer marketing.

The collaboration with brands for sponsored posts and promotions, influencers can take additional steps to ensure successful and sustainable partnerships:

Be Flexible and Open to Feedback: Brands may have specific campaign requirements or preferences. Be open to accommodating their needs and receptive to feedback to create content that meets their expectations.

Showcase Creativity and Innovation: Demonstrate your creativity by coming up with unique and innovative ways to promote the brand's products or services. Brands appreciate fresh ideas that stand out and make a lasting impression on the audience.

Leverage Storytelling: Use storytelling techniques to weave brand messages seamlessly into your content. Compelling stories can emotionally connect with your audience and leave a lasting impact, making the sponsored post more effective.

Engage with the Brand's Audience: During the collaboration period, actively engage with the brand's audience by responding to comments and messages related to the sponsored post. Your interactions contribute to the overall success of the campaign.

Create Long-Form and In-Depth Content: In addition to sponsored posts, consider creating long-form content such as blog posts, videos, or tutorials that provide in-depth information about the brand's offerings. This helps establish your authority and expertise as an influencer.

Establish Clear Guidelines: Before starting a collaboration, establish clear guidelines and expectations with the brand. Define deliverables, posting schedules, and any exclusivity clauses to avoid any misunderstandings later on.

Showcase Brand Integration: Integrate the brand organically into your regular content. This not only reinforces the brand's presence but also showcases a genuine connection between the brand and your personal brand.

Provide Value to Your Audience: Always prioritize the value you provide to your audience. Align sponsored content with your audience's interests and needs, ensuring that they find the collaboration beneficial and relevant.

Stay Compliant with Advertising Regulations: Adhere to advertising regulations and guidelines set by relevant authorities in your region. Clearly disclose sponsored content to maintain transparency with your audience.

Build Credibility and Trust: Consistently deliver high-quality sponsored posts and promotions. Building credibility with your audience establishes trust and enhances your value as a brand partner.

Seek Authentic Partnerships: Collaborate with brands that genuinely resonate with your interests and values. Authentic partnerships lead to more meaningful collaborations and contribute to your overall brand authenticity.

Collaborating with brands for sponsored posts and promotions is an opportunity for influencers to monetize their social media presence while providing value to their audience and brand partners. By showcasing creativity, authenticity, and professionalism, influencers can attract brands seeking to leverage their influence for impactful marketing campaigns.

Staying true to your niche, engaging with the brand's audience, and delivering compelling content are key factors in fostering successful and long-lasting brand collaborations. As influencers continue to build their reputation and credibility, they open doors to more significant opportunities and partnerships with brands in the dynamic landscape of influencer marketing.

9. Integrating ChatGPT-4 into Existing Passive Income Strategies

As AI technology continues to advance, the integration of more powerful language models like ChatGPT-4 opens up new possibilities for enhancing existing passive income strategies. In this chapter, we will explore how entrepreneurs and content creators can leverage ChatGPT-4 to optimize their passive income streams and embrace innovative approaches to generating revenue.

Enhancing Content Creation:

ChatGPT-4's improved language understanding and generation capabilities allow for the creation of even more engaging and high-quality content. Content creators can leverage this technology to produce blog posts, articles, and social media content that resonates better with their audience, ultimately driving more traffic and ad revenue.

Improving SEO and Keyword Research:

Integrating ChatGPT-4 into keyword research tools can result in more accurate and relevant keyword suggestions. With improved language understanding, the model can identify long-tail keywords and search queries that align better with users' intentions, leading to higher rankings and increased organic traffic.

Personalizing User Experiences:

ChatGPT-4's ability to analyze user interactions and preferences enables businesses to offer personalized user experiences. By tailoring content recommendations, product suggestions, and marketing messages to individual users, businesses can boost customer satisfaction and loyalty.

Chatbot-driven Customer Support:

ChatGPT-4's advanced natural language processing allows for more sophisticated chatbot implementations. Integrating the model into customer support systems enables businesses to provide quicker and more accurate responses, enhancing customer satisfaction and retention.

Generating Automated Reports:

For businesses that rely on data analysis and reporting, ChatGPT-4 can automate the process of generating reports. By summarizing data and presenting key insights in natural language, the model streamlines decision-making processes and saves time for entrepreneurs.

Streamlining Email Marketing:

Integrating ChatGPT-4 into email marketing platforms enables businesses to craft more personalized and persuasive email campaigns. The model can help generate compelling subject lines, email content, and calls-to-action, leading to higher open and conversion rates.

Optimizing Social Media Engagement:

ChatGPT-4's enhanced social media insights can provide valuable data on audience behavior, content performance, and trending topics. Leveraging this information, content creators can create more shareable and viral content, expanding their social media reach and engagement.

Content Monetization Strategies:

With ChatGPT-4's assistance, content creators can explore new content monetization strategies. By generating exclusive premium content, online courses, or personalized content subscriptions, creators can diversify their income streams and reach a wider audience.

Data-Driven Investment Decisions:

Investors can leverage ChatGPT-4 for advanced data analysis and predictive modeling. By analyzing market trends, financial data, and economic indicators, the model can help investors make data-driven investment decisions to enhance their passive income from investments.

Identifying Emerging Passive Income Opportunities:

ChatGPT-4's ability to analyze market trends and consumer behavior can help entrepreneurs identify emerging passive income opportunities. Whether it's exploring new niches, product ideas, or investment trends, the model can provide valuable insights for business growth.

Conclusion:

Integrating ChatGPT-4 into existing passive income strategies presents an exciting opportunity for entrepreneurs and content creators to optimize their revenue streams. By harnessing the model's advanced language capabilities, businesses can enhance content creation, improve user experiences, streamline operations, and explore new monetization avenues.

As AI technology continues to evolve, staying informed about the latest advancements and best practices is essential for leveraging ChatGPT-4 effectively. By embracing this cutting-edge tool, businesses and individuals can stay at the forefront of passive income generation and achieve greater success in their respective ventures.

Upgrading current AI-based systems to ChatGPT 4

Upgrading current AI-based systems to ChatGPT-4 offers significant advantages, considering the model's enhanced language understanding, generation capabilities, and improved performance. Here's a step-by-step guide to effectively upgrade existing AI systems to leverage ChatGPT-4:

Understand ChatGPT-4 Capabilities:

Before proceeding with the upgrade, thoroughly research and understand the specific capabilities and improvements of ChatGPT-4 compared to the previous AI model. Familiarize yourself with the enhanced features, including language understanding, multitasking, and contextual understanding.

Data Collection and Preparation:

Review and update the dataset used to train the existing AI system. Ensure that the data is relevant, diverse, and up-to-date. To optimize the benefits of ChatGPT-4, consider augmenting the dataset with additional information and examples.

Fine-tuning the Model:

ChatGPT-4 can be fine-tuned for specific tasks or domains to achieve better performance and accuracy. Fine-tuning involves training the model on task-specific data or custom datasets related to the target application. This process ensures that the model adapts to the specific context of the existing AI system.

Implement Multitasking Capabilities:

Leverage ChatGPT-4's multitasking capabilities to enable the system to handle multiple tasks simultaneously. This can significantly improve system efficiency and response times, making it more versatile and adaptable.

Upgrade Infrastructure and Compute Power:

Ensure that your existing infrastructure and compute resources can handle the increased demands of ChatGPT-4. The model may require more computational power and memory, so upgrading hardware or opting for cloud-based solutions may be necessary.

Update APIs and Integrations:

If the existing AI system integrates with other applications or platforms through APIs, ensure that these integrations are updated to support ChatGPT-4. Verify compatibility and make necessary changes to maintain seamless functionality.

Conduct Thorough Testing:

Thoroughly test the upgraded system to ensure that it performs as expected. Test for accuracy, responsiveness, and overall system performance. Address any issues or bugs that arise during testing.

Monitor Performance and Fine-tune:

After deployment, continuously monitor the performance of the upgraded AI system. Collect user feedback and data to identify areas for improvement and fine-tuning. Iteratively enhance the system to achieve optimal results.

Address Ethical Considerations:

As AI systems become more advanced, it's crucial to address ethical considerations related to data privacy, bias, and potential unintended consequences. Review and update the existing AI system's ethical guidelines to align with the use of ChatGPT-4.

Stay Updated and Embrace New Features:

AI technology is continually evolving. Stay informed about updates and new features of ChatGPT-4. Embrace these advancements to keep your AI-based system at the cutting edge and leverage the latest innovations.

Upgrading current AI-based systems to ChatGPT-4 opens up exciting possibilities for enhanced language understanding, multitasking, and improved performance. By following the steps mentioned above, businesses and developers can effectively integrate ChatGPT-4 into their existing AI systems and benefit from the model's advanced capabilities. With continuous monitoring, fine-tuning, and ethical considerations, the upgraded AI system can stay at the forefront of AI technology and deliver valuable outcomes across various applications and industries.

Businesses and developers can take further steps to optimize the integration and maximize the benefits of the advanced language model:

Leverage Pre-trained Models:

ChatGPT-4 comes pre-trained on vast amounts of data, which gives it a strong foundation for various language tasks. Utilize these pre-trained capabilities to speed up development and enhance the performance of your AI system. Fine-tuning the model on domain-specific data can further enhance its effectiveness.

Implement Transfer Learning:

Transfer learning is a powerful technique that allows you to leverage knowledge learned from one task to improve performance on another. Consider using transfer learning to fine-tune ChatGPT-4 on relevant data from your existing AI system to boost its proficiency in specific tasks.

Manage Costs and Resource Usage:

ChatGPT-4 is a highly advanced language model, and utilizing its full capabilities may come with increased computational costs. Ensure that your infrastructure and resources can handle the higher demands. Optimize resource usage by fine-tuning only the necessary parts of the model and considering cost-effective cloud computing solutions.

Integrate Feedback Loops:

Set up feedback loops to collect user feedback on the performance of the upgraded AI system. User insights can help identify areas for improvement, refine user experience, and uncover potential issues that may need addressing.

Enhance Natural Language Understanding:

ChatGPT-4's superior natural language understanding can be leveraged to enhance user interactions. Implement conversational AI features that allow users to engage in more dynamic and context-aware conversations with the system.

Optimize for Accessibility:

Ensure that the upgraded AI system is accessible to all users, including those with disabilities. Implement features such as voice commands, text-to-speech, and keyboard navigation to make the system user-friendly and inclusive.

Scale Responsibly:

As the upgraded AI system gains traction and user base, be prepared to scale your infrastructure to meet growing demands. Plan for scalability to maintain smooth user experiences during peak usage.

Address Security and Privacy:

Review and update your existing security and privacy protocols to align with the use of ChatGPT-4. Protect user data, ensure data privacy compliance, and address potential security risks associated with the upgraded system.

Monitor Performance Metrics:

Continuously monitor key performance metrics to gauge the effectiveness of ChatGPT-4 within your existing AI system. Metrics such as accuracy, response time, user engagement, and user satisfaction can provide valuable insights for further enhancements.

Stay Informed About Updates:

Stay informed about updates, advancements, and new features in the AI landscape. Regularly check for updates from the model's developers and the wider AI community to stay at the cutting edge of AI technology.

Integrating ChatGPT-4 into existing AI-based systems presents a significant opportunity to elevate performance, enhance user experiences, and unlock new possibilities for businesses and developers. By leveraging pre-trained models, fine-tuning, and transfer learning, organizations can maximize the benefits of the advanced language model.

Managing costs, optimizing resource usage, and addressing security and privacy concerns are crucial steps in ensuring a successful and responsible upgrade. Regularly monitoring performance metrics and staying informed about AI advancements will enable businesses to continuously refine and improve their AI-based systems, staying at the forefront of AI innovation. The integration of ChatGPT-4 represents a significant step forward in advancing AI capabilities and driving greater value across various industries and applications.

Maximizing earnings with the new capabilities of ChatGPT 4

Maximizing earnings with the new capabilities of ChatGPT-4 opens up exciting opportunities for businesses, content creators, and entrepreneurs. By harnessing the advanced language understanding, multitasking, and context-aware features of ChatGPT-4, individuals and organizations can optimize their passive income strategies and revenue streams. Here are effective ways to maximize earnings with ChatGPT-4:

Enhanced Content Monetization:

With ChatGPT-4's improved language generation capabilities, content creators can produce high-quality, engaging, and valuable content. By offering premium content subscriptions, online courses, or exclusive access to AI-generated content, creators can attract more paying subscribers and diversify their income streams.

Personalized Marketing Campaigns:

Leverage ChatGPT-4's ability to analyze user interactions and preferences to create personalized marketing campaigns. Tailor product recommendations, discounts, and offers based on individual user behavior to increase conversion rates and drive higher sales.

Streamlined Customer Support:

Implement ChatGPT-4-powered chatbots for customer support to provide immediate and accurate responses to customer inquiries. By enhancing the customer support experience, businesses can boost customer satisfaction and retain more loyal customers.

Data-Driven Investment Decisions:

Investors can leverage ChatGPT-4's advanced data analysis capabilities to make data-driven investment decisions. Analyzing market trends, financial data, and economic indicators, investors can optimize their investment strategies and potentially increase passive income from investments.

Niche Market Exploration:

Utilize ChatGPT-4's ability to identify emerging trends and niche markets. By tapping into untapped markets and offering unique products or services, businesses can establish themselves as industry leaders and capture a more targeted audience.

Optimize SEO and Content Strategy:

ChatGPT-4 can provide valuable insights into trending topics, long-tail keywords, and user intent. By optimizing SEO strategies and content creation based on AI-generated insights, businesses can increase organic traffic, leading to higher ad revenue and affiliate earnings.

Efficient Email Marketing:

Integrate ChatGPT-4 into email marketing campaigns to generate personalized and persuasive email content. AI-generated subject lines and content can improve open rates, click-through rates, and ultimately drive more sales and conversions.

Upselling and Cross-Selling:

Leverage ChatGPT-4 to identify upselling and cross-selling opportunities based on user behavior and purchase history. Recommending relevant products or services can increase the average order value and boost overall earnings.

ChatGPT-Powered Affiliate Marketing:

Content creators and influencers can use ChatGPT-4 to optimize their affiliate marketing efforts. By generating persuasive affiliate content and recommendations, influencers can attract more clicks and conversions, increasing their affiliate earnings.

Expansion into New Content Formats:

Explore new content formats enabled by ChatGPT-4, such as interactive quizzes, AR/VR experiences, or voice-enabled content. Innovating with new formats can attract a broader audience and potentially lead to additional revenue streams.

Maximizing earnings with ChatGPT-4 requires a strategic approach to leverage its advanced language capabilities effectively. Content creators, businesses, and investors can optimize content monetization, marketing campaigns, customer support, and investment decisions through the integration of ChatGPT-4.

By staying informed about AI advancements, embracing data-driven strategies, and continuously refining their approach, individuals and organizations can unlock the full potential of ChatGPT-4 and achieve greater financial success in the dynamic landscape of passive income generation.

Here are additional strategies for businesses and content creators:

Dynamic Pricing Strategies:

Utilize ChatGPT-4's ability to analyze market trends and consumer behavior to implement dynamic pricing strategies. By adjusting prices in real-time based on demand and user interactions, businesses can optimize revenue and profitability.

AI-Driven Product Recommendations:

Integrate AI-powered product recommendation engines into e-commerce platforms. By leveraging ChatGPT-4 to provide personalized product recommendations based on user preferences and behavior, businesses can increase upselling and cross-selling opportunities.

Content Licensing and Syndication:

Content creators can explore content licensing and syndication opportunities with ChatGPT-4-generated material. By licensing their AI-generated content to other platforms or publications, creators can earn additional income from their work.

Sponsored Content Optimization:

For influencers and content creators, ChatGPT-4 can help optimize sponsored content campaigns. By generating authentic and persuasive sponsored posts, influencers can attract more brands and negotiate higher sponsorship deals.

Predictive Analytics for Revenue Forecasting:

Integrate ChatGPT-4 into revenue forecasting models to make more accurate predictions about future earnings. AI-driven predictive analytics can assist businesses in making informed decisions to maximize revenue and profitability.

Real-Time Sentiment Analysis:

Implement real-time sentiment analysis using ChatGPT-4 to gauge audience reactions to marketing campaigns, product launches, or content. This helps businesses respond quickly to feedback and adjust strategies for better audience engagement.

AI-Powered A/B Testing:

Leverage ChatGPT-4 to conduct AI-powered A/B testing for marketing campaigns and website optimization. The model can analyze user responses to different variations and recommend the most effective options for maximizing conversions.

Subscription-Based Services:

Content creators can introduce subscription-based services that provide access to exclusive AI-generated content, personalized insights, or interactive experiences. Subscriptions can provide a stable and predictable income stream.

Strategic Partnerships:

Collaborate with AI developers, data scientists, or AI startups to explore innovative AI-powered solutions that align with your business goals. Strategic partnerships can lead to new revenue streams and novel applications of ChatGPT-4.

Continuous Innovation:

Embrace a culture of continuous innovation with AI. Regularly explore new features and advancements in ChatGPT-4, experiment with novel use cases, and keep your offerings fresh and relevant to the evolving needs of your audience.

Maximizing earnings with ChatGPT-4 requires a proactive and adaptive approach to leverage its cutting-edge capabilities effectively. By applying AI-driven strategies across content creation, marketing, customer support, investment, and more, businesses and content creators can optimize their passive income and revenue streams.

As AI technology continues to evolve, staying at the forefront of AI advancements and adopting a data-driven and experimental mindset will be key to unlocking the full potential of ChatGPT-4. With strategic planning, continuous innovation, and a customer-centric approach, businesses and content creators can achieve greater financial success and thrive in the ever-changing landscape of passive income generation.

Optimizing AI-driven projects for ChatGPT 4 compatibility

Optimizing AI-driven projects for ChatGPT-4 compatibility opens up new opportunities to leverage the model's advanced capabilities and enhance project performance. Whether you're a developer, business owner, or content creator, here are key steps to ensure seamless integration and maximize the benefits of ChatGPT-4:

Understand ChatGPT-4 Features:

Before optimization, familiarize yourself with ChatGPT-4's features and improvements. Understand how its enhanced language understanding, multitasking, and contextual capabilities can enhance your project.

Data Preparation and Augmentation:

Review and update your dataset to ensure it aligns with ChatGPT-4's requirements. Consider augmenting the data with additional information to improve the model's performance and adaptability.

Fine-Tuning for Specific Tasks:

Fine-tune ChatGPT-4 for your project's specific tasks or domain. By fine-tuning the model on relevant data, you can tailor its behavior and ensure it aligns with the context of your project.

Compatibility with APIs and Interfaces:

Verify that your project's APIs and interfaces are compatible with ChatGPT-4. Make necessary changes to ensure seamless integration and communication with the model.

Performance Optimization:

Assess your project's computational requirements and performance. Optimize resource usage and infrastructure to handle the increased demands of ChatGPT-4 effectively.

Address Privacy and Security Concerns:

Review and update your project's privacy and security protocols to align with ChatGPT-4. Ensure that user data is protected and compliance with data privacy regulations is maintained.

User Experience Enhancement:

Implement ChatGPT-4 to enhance user experiences. Whether it's providing more accurate recommendations, dynamic responses, or personalized interactions, focus on improving user satisfaction.

AI Governance and Ethics:

Incorporate AI governance and ethical considerations into your project. Ensure transparency in AI-generated content, and address any potential biases or unintended consequences.

Scaling for Growth:

Plan for scalability as your project gains traction and user base. Ensure that your infrastructure and resources can handle increased user interactions and demand.

Continuous Monitoring and Iteration:

Regularly monitor ChatGPT-4's performance within your project. Collect user feedback and iterate on the model to make continuous improvements based on user insights.

Documentation and Training:

Provide comprehensive documentation and training materials for developers and users. Empower your team with the knowledge needed to effectively utilize ChatGPT-4 within the project.

Integration with AI Workflow:

Integrate ChatGPT-4 into your project's AI workflow seamlessly. Ensure smooth data flow and communication between different components of the project.

Regular Model Updates:

Stay informed about updates and advancements in ChatGPT-4. Regularly update your model to leverage the latest improvements and features.

Multilingual Support:

Explore multilingual capabilities of ChatGPT-4 to expand your project's reach to a global audience. Consider offering content and interactions in multiple languages.

Collaboration and Knowledge Sharing:

Engage with the AI community to share knowledge and best practices for optimizing projects with ChatGPT-4. Collaborate with other developers and businesses to learn from each other's experiences.

Optimizing AI-driven projects for ChatGPT-4 compatibility requires a systematic approach that includes understanding the model's features, fine-tuning for specific tasks, addressing security and privacy concerns, and enhancing user experiences. By following these steps and staying informed about AI advancements, you can seamlessly integrate ChatGPT-4 into your projects and unlock its full potential for enhanced performance and innovation. Embrace continuous improvement and a user-centric approach to thrive in the dynamic landscape of AI-driven projects with ChatGPT-4.

10. The Future of ChatGPT and Passive Income

As AI technology continues to evolve, the future of ChatGPT holds exciting possibilities for the world of passive income. In this chapter, we explore the potential advancements in ChatGPT and how they will shape the landscape of passive income strategies for businesses, content creators, investors, and entrepreneurs.

ChatGPT Advancements:

The future of ChatGPT is likely to see continuous advancements in language understanding, context-awareness, and multitasking capabilities. As models become even more sophisticated, they will offer better performance and accuracy, enabling businesses to generate higher-quality content and personalized user experiences.

Increased Integration:

ChatGPT is expected to be seamlessly integrated into various platforms and applications, making AI-powered functionalities more accessible to businesses and content creators. From e-commerce websites to social media platforms, AI-driven insights will become an essential part of content creation, marketing, and customer support strategies.

Natural Conversational Interfaces:

Future iterations of ChatGPT might focus on enhancing natural conversational interfaces. This means AI chatbots and virtual assistants will engage in more dynamic, context-aware conversations with users, leading to more personalized recommendations and improved user interactions.

Expansion of Multilingual Support:

ChatGPT is likely to see further expansion of multilingual support, enabling businesses and content creators to connect with global audiences seamlessly. This will open doors to new markets and opportunities for passive income generation on a global scale.

Voice-Enabled Passive Income:

With the rise of voice assistants, ChatGPT's future may involve catering to voice-enabled passive income strategies. From voice-generated content to AI-powered voice commerce, businesses can leverage voice technology to drive revenue and enhance user experiences.

AI-Driven Predictive Insights:

Future ChatGPT models may provide businesses with AI-driven predictive insights to identify emerging trends, customer preferences, and market opportunities. Armed with such insights, entrepreneurs can proactively capitalize on potential passive income streams.

Autonomous AI Business Models:

The future may see the emergence of autonomous AI business models that leverage ChatGPT to generate and manage content, conduct customer interactions, and optimize revenue streams without human intervention. This can lead to passive income generation with minimal human effort.

AI for Investment Decisions:

Investors may heavily rely on AI-driven insights from ChatGPT to make informed investment decisions. ChatGPT could analyze vast amounts of data, predict market trends, and provide real-time recommendations for optimizing investment portfolios.

AI-Enhanced Niche Websites:

ChatGPT's future capabilities can revolutionize niche websites, enabling them to provide highly personalized and valuable content to visitors. AI-driven recommendations and content creation will boost engagement and ad revenue for niche websites.

Embracing AI-First Strategies:

Businesses and content creators may adopt AI-first strategies, where AI-driven insights and applications become the foundation of their passive income approaches. From content creation to customer engagement, AI will play a central role in maximizing earnings.

The future of ChatGPT promises to reshape the landscape of passive income strategies for businesses, content creators, investors, and entrepreneurs. With advancements in language understanding, context-awareness, and multilingual support, ChatGPT will become a critical tool for generating high-quality content, optimizing marketing campaigns, and providing personalized user experiences.

As AI becomes more integrated into various industries, passive income opportunities will expand, and new revenue streams will emerge. Embracing AI-driven strategies, staying at the forefront of technological advancements, and continuously innovating will be essential for leveraging ChatGPT's future capabilities to achieve financial success in the evolving world of passive income. Whether you are a content creator seeking to monetize your expertise or an investor looking for data-driven insights, ChatGPT will play a pivotal role in driving your passive income endeavors forward.

Exploring Emerging Industries and Trends for AI Application

As AI technology continues to advance, it is revolutionizing various industries and creating new opportunities for application. Here are some emerging industries and trends where AI is making a significant impact:

Healthcare and Medicine:

AI is transforming healthcare by aiding in medical diagnoses, drug discovery, and personalized treatments. Machine learning algorithms analyze vast amounts of patient data to identify patterns, predict diseases, and recommend personalized treatment plans. AI-powered medical imaging is also improving the accuracy of diagnostics, helping healthcare professionals make better decisions.

Autonomous Vehicles:

The automotive industry is witnessing a rapid shift towards autonomous vehicles. AI-driven technologies, such as computer vision and deep learning algorithms, enable vehicles to perceive their surroundings, navigate through traffic, and make real-time driving decisions. Self-driving cars are expected to enhance road safety, reduce accidents, and revolutionize transportation.

Education and E-Learning:

AI is transforming education through personalized learning experiences. Adaptive learning platforms use AI algorithms to understand students' strengths and weaknesses, offering customized study materials and exercises. Natural language processing enables AI-powered chatbots to provide instant assistance and tutoring, enhancing the overall learning process.

Agriculture:

AI is being applied to precision agriculture, helping farmers optimize crop yields, reduce resource wastage, and make data-driven decisions. Drones equipped with AI-powered sensors monitor crop health, while AI-driven analytics provide insights on soil conditions and pest management.

Finance and Fintech:

In the financial sector, AI is being used for fraud detection, risk assessment, and algorithmic trading. Chatbots and virtual assistants improve customer support and streamline financial services. Fintech companies are leveraging AI to offer personalized financial advice and investment strategies.

Entertainment and Gaming:

AI is enhancing the entertainment and gaming industries through realistic graphics, immersive experiences, and intelligent gameplay. AI algorithms are used to create lifelike characters, optimize game mechanics, and personalize user experiences based on player behavior.

Environmental Sustainability:

AI is playing a crucial role in environmental conservation and sustainability efforts. AI-powered sensors and monitoring systems are used to track wildlife populations, monitor pollution levels, and manage renewable energy sources more efficiently.

Cybersecurity:

The increasing complexity of cyber threats demands advanced security measures. AI-driven cybersecurity solutions use machine learning to detect anomalies, identify potential breaches, and respond to security incidents in real-time.

Retail and E-Commerce:

AI is transforming the retail industry with personalized product recommendations, dynamic pricing, and chatbots for customer support. AI-powered visual search enables customers to find products based on images, enhancing the shopping experience.

Human Resources:

AI is streamlining HR processes by automating candidate screening, conducting sentiment analysis in employee feedback, and predicting employee attrition. AI-powered tools aid in talent acquisition, workforce management, and employee engagement.

The application of AI is rapidly expanding across various industries, creating exciting opportunities for innovation and growth. From healthcare to finance, education to entertainment, AI is revolutionizing how businesses operate and deliver value to customers. As AI technology continues to evolve, we can expect even more groundbreaking applications that will shape the future of industries worldwide. Entrepreneurs and businesses that embrace AI-driven strategies will stay at the forefront of these emerging trends, driving success and sustainability in the ever-changing landscape of AI application.

Strategies for staying ahead in the rapidly evolving AI landscape

Staying ahead in the rapidly evolving AI landscape requires a proactive and adaptive approach. As technology advances, new opportunities and challenges arise. Here are some strategies to keep pace and remain at the forefront of the AI revolution:

Continuous Learning and Skill Development:

Stay updated with the latest developments in AI by engaging in continuous learning. Take online courses, attend workshops, and participate in industry conferences to enhance your knowledge and skills in AI technologies and methodologies.

Embrace Experimentation and Innovation:

Be open to experimentation and innovation. Test new AI tools, frameworks, and models to understand their potential applications. Embrace a culture of innovation within your organization and encourage team members to explore novel AI-driven solutions.

Collaborate with the AI Community:

Engage with the AI community, including researchers, developers, and businesses. Collaborate on projects, share knowledge, and participate in AI-focused forums and discussions to gain valuable insights and stay connected to the latest trends.

AI-First Approach:

Adopt an AI-first approach in your business strategies. Integrate AI technologies and AI-driven insights into your decision-making processes, product development, and customer interactions. Embrace AI as a fundamental element of your operations.

Invest in Data and Data Analytics:

Data is the backbone of AI. Invest in data collection, storage, and management infrastructure. Leverage data analytics to gain meaningful insights that can inform AI applications and drive data-driven decision-making.

Ethical and Responsible AI Implementation:

Stay informed about ethical AI practices and regulatory guidelines. Implement AI systems responsibly, ensuring transparency, fairness, and privacy in AI-driven solutions. Address any potential biases and unintended consequences of AI algorithms.

Partner with AI Experts:

If your organization lacks in-house AI expertise, consider partnering with AI experts or hiring AI consultants. Collaborating with experienced professionals can accelerate your AI initiatives and ensure optimal use of AI technologies.

Monitor Industry Trends:

Keep a close eye on industry trends and emerging AI applications. Monitor the activities of competitors and leaders in your domain. Analyze how AI is being integrated into your industry and explore ways to leverage AI for a competitive edge.

Agility and Flexibility:

In a rapidly changing AI landscape, be agile and flexible in adapting to new opportunities and challenges. Be willing to pivot and adjust your AI strategies based on market demands and technological advancements.

Invest in AI Infrastructure:

Ensure that your organization has the necessary computational resources and AI infrastructure to support AI-driven projects effectively. Cloud-based solutions and AI accelerators can help scale AI initiatives efficiently.

Staying ahead in the rapidly evolving AI landscape requires a forward-thinking mindset, continuous learning, and a strong commitment to innovation. Embrace AI technologies as a transformative force, and explore ways to integrate AI into various aspects of your business and operations. By being proactive, collaborative, and adaptable, you can navigate the dynamic AI landscape successfully and position your organization for sustained growth and success in the AI-driven future.

Conclusion

The ChatGPT Passive Income Playbook has explored the vast potential of passive income generation using AI-powered technologies, specifically focusing on the groundbreaking capabilities of ChatGPT-4. Throughout the chapters, we have delved into various strategies and applications that can lead to financial freedom and success in the dynamic world of passive income.

ChatGPT-4's advanced language understanding, multitasking, and context-aware features offer tremendous opportunities for businesses, content creators, investors, and entrepreneurs to optimize their earnings and create new revenue streams.

From leveraging ChatGPT for content creation, social media engagement, and e-commerce sales, to building niche websites and AI-powered chatbots for customer support, the playbook has provided a comprehensive guide to harnessing the power of AI for passive income.

As AI technology continues to evolve, the future of ChatGPT and its applications holds even more promise. From emerging industries to innovative trends, staying ahead in the rapidly evolving AI landscape demands continuous learning, collaboration with the AI community, and a commitment to ethical and responsible AI implementation.

By adopting an AI-first approach, embracing innovation, and investing in AI infrastructure, businesses and individuals can position themselves at the forefront of the AI-driven revolution and unlock unparalleled opportunities for financial success.

The future of passive income is dynamic and ever-evolving, and those who embrace AI-powered strategies and stay informed about the latest advancements will thrive in this new era of innovation. Whether you're a content creator, investor, or business owner, the ChatGPT Passive Income Playbook equips you with the knowledge and insights to achieve financial freedom and excel in the exciting world of AI-driven passive income.

Now, armed with the secrets of ChatGPT and its limitless potential, it is up to you to embark on your journey to financial freedom and chart a path towards a prosperous future powered by the groundbreaking capabilities of AI. Embrace the AI revolution, seize opportunities, and let the ChatGPT Passive Income Playbook be your guide to unlocking the boundless potential of passive income generation in the age of AI. The future awaits, and the possibilities are limitless.

www.ingramcontent.com/pod-product-compliance
Lightning Source LLC
LaVergne TN
LVHW080527210926
848481LV00022B/3585
* 9 7 9 8 2 2 3 9 8 1 6 2 6 *